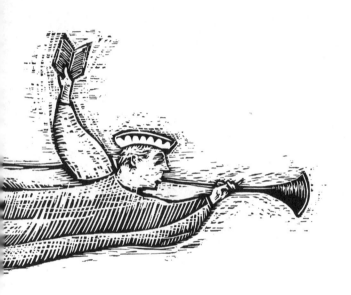

Alma 30–63: *a brief theological introduction*

This publication was made possible by generous support from the Laura F. Willes Center for Book of Mormon Studies, part of the Neal A. Maxwell Institute for Religious Scholarship at Brigham Young University.

Published by the Neal A. Maxwell Institute for Religious Scholarship, Brigham Young University, Provo, Utah. The copyright for the 2013 text of The Book of Mormon is held by The Church of Jesus Christ of Latter-day Saints, Salt Lake City, Utah; that text is quoted throughout, and used by permission.

Printed in the United States of America

ISBN: 978-0-8425-0020-3

LIBRARY OF CONGRESS CONTROL NUMBER: 2020902747

Alma 30–63

a brief theological introduction

BRIGHAM YOUNG UNIVERSITY

NEAL A. MAXWELL INSTITUTE

PROVO, UTAH

Mark A. Wrathall

EDITORS

General Editors
J. Spencer Fluhman, Philip L. Barlow

Series Editors
D. Morgan Davis, James E. Faulconer,
Kristine Haglund, Joseph M. Spencer,
Rosalynde Frandsen Welch

Chief Editorial Assistants
Blair Dee Hodges, Camille Messick

Editorial Assistants
Anna Allred, Lilia Brown, Alexander Christensen,
Isana Garcia, Reagan Graff, Tessa Hauglid, Sol Lee,
Bruce Lott, Jessica Mitton, Olivia DeMordaunt,
Ryder Seamons, Sandra Shurtleff

SERIES AUTHORS

1st Nephi	Joseph M. Spencer
2nd Nephi	Terryl Givens
Jacob	Deidre Nicole Green
Enos, Jarom, Omni	Sharon J. Harris
Mosiah	James E. Faulconer
Alma 1–29	Kylie Nielson Turley
Alma 30–63	Mark A. Wrathall
Helaman	Kimberly Matheson Berkey
3rd, 4th Nephi	Daniel Becerra
Mormon	Adam S. Miller
Ether	Rosalynde Frandsen Welch
Moroni	David F. Holland

The Book of Mormon: brief theological introductions series seeks Christ in scripture by combining intellectual rigor and the disciple's yearning for holiness. It answers Elder Neal A. Maxwell's call to explore the book's "divine architecture": "There is so much more in the Book of Mormon than we have yet discovered. The book's divine architecture and rich furnishings will increasingly unfold to our view, further qualifying it as *'a marvelous work and a wonder.'* (Isaiah 29:14) . . . All the rooms in this mansion need to be explored, whether by valued traditional scholars or by those at the cutting edge. Each plays a role, and one LDS scholar cannot say to the other, *'I have no need of thee.'*" [1] (1 Corinthians 12:21)

For some time, faithful scholars have explored the book's textual history, reception, historicity, literary quality, and more. This series focuses particularly on theology—the scholarly practice of exploring a scriptural text's implications and its lens on God's work in the world. Series volumes invite Latter-day Saints to discover additional dimensions of this treasured text but leave to prophets and apostles their unique role of declaring its definitive official doctrines. In this case, theology, as opposed to authoritative doctrine, relates to the original sense of the term as, literally, reasoned "God talk." The word also designates a well-developed academic field, but it is the more general sense of the term that most often applies here. By engaging each scriptural book's theology on its own terms, this series explores the spiritual and intellectual force of the ideas appearing in the Latter-day Saints' "keystone" scripture.

Series authors and editors possess specialized professional training that informs their work but, significantly, each takes Christ as theology's proper end because he is the proper end of all scripture and all reflection on it. We, too, "talk of Christ, we rejoice in Christ, we preach of Christ . . . that our children may know to what source they may look for a remission of their sins" (2 Nephi 25:26). Moreover, while experts in the modern disciplines of philosophy, theology, literature, and history, series authors and editors also work explicitly within the context of personal and institutional commitments both to Christian discipleship and to the Church of Jesus Christ of Latter-day Saints. These volumes are not official Church publications but can be best understood in light of these deep commitments. And because we acknowledge that scripture demands far more than intellectual experimentation, we call readers' attention to the processes of conversion and sanctification at play on virtually every scriptural page.

Individual series authors offer unique approaches but, taken together, they model a joint invitation to readers to engage scripture in their own way. No single approach to theology or scriptural interpretation commands preeminence in these volumes. No volume pretends to be the final word on theological reflection for its part of the Book of Mormon. Varied perspectives and methodologies are evident throughout. This is intentional. In addition, though we recognize love for the Book of Mormon is a "given" for most Latter-day Saint readers, we also share the conviction that, like the gospel of Jesus Christ itself, the Book of Mormon is inexhaustible.[2] These volumes invite readers to slow down and read scripture more thoughtfully and transformatively. Elder Maxwell cautioned against reading the Book of Mormon as "hurried tourists" who scarcely venture beyond "the entry hall."[3] To that end, we dedicate this series to his apostolic conviction that there is always more to learn from the Book of Mormon and much to be gained from our faithful search for Christ in its pages.

— The Editors

Contents

Introduction

The book of Alma is a demanding book. If you don't feel challenged by it—challenged to change your priorities, your everyday practices, and your worldly preoccupations—you probably have not understood it. Your understanding of scriptures is manifest in what you do in response to them, not what you say or think about them. In the end, an authentic understanding of scriptures has very little to do with being able to derive from them a rationally defensible theology.

The authors and editors of the book of Alma don't articulate and defend theories about God. They describe their firsthand experiences—experiences of a life devoted to the service of God. For them, this service meant working tirelessly to establish communities tied together in love, mercy, humility, and joy. When they do teach doctrines, they always do it to correct bad practices—practices that cut us off from God and each other. They thus approach doctrinal teaching very differently than a theologian would. Where a theologian would construct an argument, they appeal to the confirmation of the spirit or the promises contained in the scriptures. Even when engaged in a doctrinal dispute (explicitly against Korihor, for instance, and implicitly against the Zoramites), they don't try to resolve the dispute by discovering flaws or contradictions in the teachings of their opponents. In a word, Alma and Amulek are not theologians.

I am not a theologian either. I am no more interested than Alma was in developing theories about God or in demonstrating through rational argumentation that God exists or possesses certain properties. But I am a philosopher. Philosophers have developed certain techniques for analyzing ideas and texts. For readers unfamiliar with philosophy, the philosophical style of discourse might seem unnatural or alienating. I ask the reader to be patient with this; it can be a bit like learning a new language. If you stick with it, you'll find that philosophical modes of analysis are very good at articulating and carefully laying out the precise meaning of a text. While Alma and Amulek were not theologians, they were sophisticated teachers of doctrine. There is a rigorous structure to their teachings that all too often gets overlooked, and, as I hope to show, philosophical modes of analysis can help us recognize this.

I've structured this book in three parts. This echoes the threefold structure of Christian life as Alma understands it. The followers of Christ live the present moment as stretched out between a constant and faithful remembrance of the past, and a hopeful anticipation of the future. Our past—the event that initiated us into the Christian community—is captured in the central metaphor of the planting of the seed. Part I centers on understanding how this planting, and our response to it, can shape our characters and our dispositions. In Part II, I look at Alma's account of the Christian present as a "probationary" or a "preparatory" state, a time for us to prove and improve our character (Alma 42:4, 10). The *now* of the follower of Christ is thus an exercise in the literal sense. It requires exertion, movement, and the use of all our faculties as we engage with the people and things around us. In particular, today is devoted to practicing mercy, learning both how to receive mercy and how to give it. The Christian "now" is absorbed in works of love. In Part III, my focus is the Christian future—the anticipation of meeting God and the hope of a restoration.

The three dimensions of the time of Christian life, however, are not something that happen in a sequence. If we are doing it right, we are continually nourishing the seed that was once planted, and it is already bearing the fruit we hope for.

PART I

Alma's Sermon on the Seed

The "church of God" was established in Zarahemla during the reign of King Mosiah (see Mosiah 25:19–24). The central doctrine of the new church was the doctrine of the coming of Christ—that is, the doctrine that Christ would in the future come to redeem his people through his suffering, death, and resurrection (see Mosiah 18:2).

In the first decades after its establishment, however, the new church faced a recurring challenge: waves of articulate and persuasive teachers who disputed the core doctrine of the church. For instance, the high priest Alma had to deal with a particularly charismatic man, "a man of many words," a "very wicked and idolatrous man" who "caus[ed] much dissension among the people." I'm speaking, of course, of Alma's own son:

> one of the sons of Alma was numbered among them [the unbelievers], he being called Alma, after his father; nevertheless, he became a very wicked and an idolatrous man. And he was a man of many words, and did speak much flattery to the people; therefore he led many of the people to do after the manner of his iniquities. And he became a great hinderment to the prosperity of the church of God; stealing away the hearts of the people; causing much dissension among the people; giving a chance for the enemy of God to exercise his power over them. (Mosiah 27:8–9)

In part 2 of this book, we'll look in more detail at the conversion of Alma the Younger, 🖝 and at his transformation into the leader of the church of God. In this part, however, I want to focus on some of the various forms

🖝 All subsequent references to Alma refer to Alma the Younger, not his father of the same name. Kylie Turley notes that the Book of Mormon never uses Alma the Younger as a name-title. It has only been introduced in modern study helps, such as chapter headings or general church parlance. For more on the implications of "the younger" for our understanding of Alma, see her volume in this series (*Alma 1–29: a brief theological introduction*).

of apostasy that Alma himself faced after he replaced his father as the high priest of the church of God (see Alma 4:4).

The core teaching of the nascent church, as we've noted, was the teaching that a Christ would come in the future to redeem his people. The recurring attacks on this doctrine led to schism and apostasy that sometimes flared into persecution and violence. The book of Alma begins with a confrontation between Alma and an apostate preacher—Nehor. In ensuing chapters, Alma sets out on a journey with a goal: to "pull down, by the word of God, all the pride and craftiness and all the contentions which were among his people" (Alma 4:19). This journey culminates in his encounter with the apostate Nehorites in the city of Ammonihah.

This same pattern is repeated in the second half of the book of Alma. In chapter 30, Alma confronts a charismatic apostate teacher named Korihor. In chapters 31 to 35, we follow Alma as he once again sets off on a journey to respond to growing apostasy—this time to the land of Antionum, where he preaches to the Zoramites. Although distinct from each other in most respects, Korihor and Zoram held in common a rejection of the doctrine of the coming of Christ. They each argued that the belief in a future savior was intellectually unwarranted and unjustified. These arguments turned crucially on the apostates' background assumptions about the nature of faith and knowledge. Both Korihor and the Zoramites relied heavily on their deeply held theories of the proper means and methods that should be used to acquire beliefs. "Ye cannot know of things which ye do not see," Korihor argued, "therefore ye cannot know that there shall be a Christ" (Alma 30:15). Korihor's theory of knowledge—his "epistemology"—will be the central focus in chapter 2. The Zoramites concluded that they could know that "there shall be no Christ" because they knew that God is "the same yesterday, today, and forever" (Alma 31:16–17). We'll explore the Zoramite beliefs in chapter 3. Alma, in his great Sermon on the Seed, showed that the apostates were fundamentally wrongheaded in their approach to faith. In particular, they each believed that faith needs to be grounded in knowledge or in a sure belief. As a result, they misunderstood the true character of faith and the proper relationship between faith and knowledge. "Faith is not a perfect knowledge," Alma explained (Alma 32:21, see also verse 26), and knowledge is neither the foundation of nor the end goal of a life of faith (although a kind of knowledge might be a side effect of a life of faith). We'll look at Alma's own approach to questions of faith and knowledge in chapter 4. But before all that, we'll take up in chapter 1 a more fundamental question: How, in general, should we understand concepts like *knowledge*, *belief*, and *faith*?

1

Belief, Knowledge, and Faith

Faith is the first principle of a life of discipleship. A principle is a foundation that shapes and sustains everything that is built upon it. A misunderstanding of this first principle could affect every aspect of our way of life. It's thus worth taking some time to reflect on the basic character of faith.

In everyday use, nouns like *faith*, *knowledge*, and *belief* have a broad and rather imprecise sense. All three concepts are usually understood as varieties of mentally accepting something as true. If I'm discussing English Premier League football with a friend, for instance, I might say either "I know that Chelsea will win next weekend" or "I believe that Chelsea will win next weekend" or "I have faith in Chelsea." In each case, I'm simply saying, "I hold it to be true that Chelsea will win."

This loose, everyday way of talking encourages a misunderstanding of religious faith. Here's why: The whole point of having a belief is to truly represent the state of the world. The better a belief is supported by reason and evidence, the more reliable and useful it is as a representation. When we think of religious faith as a belief, we typically think of it as the kind of belief that lacks rational support and empirical evidence. Thus an expression like "you have to take it on faith" means "you have to accept it as true, even though there is inadequate evidence to justify accepting it."

But this is not at all the way that faith is understood in the book of Alma. Faith is not about thinking the right things. It's not concerned with straightening out our beliefs about the world. As we will see, faith, for Alma, is a practical stance—a way of being poised and ready to actively respond to the world.

So to fully appreciate Alma's view of faith, we first need to rid ourselves of the idea that faith is a type of belief or that it is somehow inferior to knowledge. Toward that end, it's helpful to define our terms as clearly and precisely as possible. In section A, we'll analyze belief and knowledge (and I will, in the course of this analysis, introduce readers to philosophical modes of thinking about belief). In section B, we'll turn to an analysis of the concept of faith in the book of Alma. The distinctions we draw between belief, faith, and knowledge will equip us, in future chapters, to understand Alma's response to Korihor and the Zoramites, as well as his Sermon on the Seed.

In section A, some readers might be put off by the dry and abstract way in which philosophers and theologians talk about such matters. Those readers are free to skip to section B, where we will explore just how different faith and belief are on Alma's account. But the distinctive character of Alma's understanding of faith will be more evident to those readers who do take the trouble to work through section A.

I'll conclude this chapter, in section C, by briefly considering some hybrid attitudes that involve both a heavy cognitive commitment (as does belief) and a substantial practical commitment (as does faith). These hybrid attitudes include things like *knowing-how* and *believing in*.

section a: knowledge and belief
It is clear from the very outset of the Sermon on the Seed that Alma draws a clear distinction between belief and knowledge. "Blessed is he that believeth in the word of God," Alma declares, "without being brought to know the word, or even compelled to know, before they will

believe" (Alma 32:16). How exactly should we understand this distinction?

When philosophers analyze words and concepts, we sometimes describe them formally and abstractly to help us focus on their structure. With a clear view of their structure, we can discover differences between concepts that we wouldn't otherwise notice. This will be helpful when comparing belief to knowledge.

Both belief and knowledge involve accepting or assenting to a proposition, so we ought to define more carefully what a proposition is. A proposition is a complete thought that can be evaluated for truth or falsity. For instance,

chair

is not a proposition. Nor is

the yellow chair in my office.

But

The chair in my office is yellow

is a proposition—if I were to assert that, I would be making a claim that is capable of being true or false. (In this case, it happens to be true.) Suppose that Hannah believes the chair in my office is yellow. That means Hannah holds it to be true that the chair in my office is yellow. Now, let's abstract away the content of this particular belief so that we can focus on the structure of belief in general. We can formally represent any proposition whatsoever with the variable p. And we can formally represent people with capital letters A, B, C, and so on. So instead of saying "Hannah believes that the chair in my office is yellow," I can now formalize this idea, and capture the structure of any possible belief like this: A believes that p. And since we said that belief really amounts to a holding-to-be-true, we can formally define belief in general in this way:

A believes that p if and only if:

Ⓐ A holds it to be true that p.

Now let's work out the structure of knowledge. Knowledge differs from belief in two related respects. First, we don't normally say that someone knows something that is untrue, but we can say that someone believes something that's not true. This is because (and this is the second important distinction between belief and knowledge), knowledge is thought to involve a degree of certainty or security that belief lacks. If I'm choosing my words with care, when I say "I believe that p," this implies that I acknowledge some significant possibility that p is false. Not so when I say "I know that p." When I know something, I don't acknowledge the possibility of error. This is because I properly know something only when its truth is secured and sure.

So we can formally define knowledge in general in this way:

A knows that p if and only if:

(A) A holds it to be true that p;

(B) It is true that p;

(C) A's holding it to be true that p is secured in some appropriate way.

This securing—(C)—is emphasized in the book of Alma with the phrase "to know of a surety" (see, for example, Alma 5:45; 30:15; 32:17, 26). Philosophers today continue to argue over what it takes to "secure" a belief or achieve a "surety" regarding what one holds to be true. Alma recognizes two basic categories of knowledge: "knowing of myself" and "not knowing of myself." I'll refer to these two ways of securing knowledge as "direct" and "indirect," respectively.

Alma says that he "knows of himself" when he has a direct sensory experience of some fact. Direct sensory experience is arguably the principal means of securing knowledge in the book of Alma. It is a means accepted by those inside and outside of the church of God alike. For instance, as we'll discuss at some length in chapter

2, Korihor the anti-Christ adopts the following as his basic principle: "ye cannot know of things which ye do not see" (Alma 30:15). While Alma rejects the idea that this is the only way to secure knowledge, he too accepts direct experience as a means for securing knowledge. In fact, the Sermon on the Seed depends on it—one gains knowledge of the goodness of the seed by experiencing firsthand its effects (Alma 32:34; see chapter 4). And in his "commandments" to his son Helaman, Alma explains that "many have been born of God, and have tasted as I have tasted, and have seen eye to eye as I have seen; therefore they do know of these things of which I have spoken, as I do know" (Alma 36:26).

The second category of knowledge—indirect knowledge or knowledge "not known of myself"—is knowledge secured by the mediation of some other person or thing. Thus, for example, Alma explains to Helaman that he "know[s] that whosoever shall put their trust in God shall be supported in their trials, and their troubles, and their afflictions, and shall be lifted up at the last day" (Alma 36:3). But Alma is quick to qualify this claim: "I would not that ye think that I know of myself" (verse 4). He gives two reasons for claiming that he does not know of himself. First, he explains that "if I had not been born of God I should not have known these things" (verse 5). Thus, Alma's knowledge is causally dependent on factors beyond his or any mortal being's control, and that means he is not on his own able to secure the knowledge. Secondly, he does not know of himself because "God has, by the mouth of his holy angel, made these things known unto me" (verse 5). More generally, we could say that all knowledge grounded in testimony is knowledge secured by the mediation of some other thing. *Testimony* is used here in a broad sense to include the witness of others (other people, angels, and the scriptures).

Interestingly, Alma treats the witness of the Holy Spirit not as a form of testimony but rather as a kind of direct experience of the truth of some fact. For instance, he claims:

> I know of myself that whatsoever I shall say unto you, concerning that which is to come, is true; and I say unto you, that I know that Jesus Christ shall come (Alma 5:48).

Now Alma doesn't have direct sensory experience that Jesus Christ will come, so it doesn't seem to qualify as "knowledge of myself." But Alma explains:

> I have fasted and prayed many days that I might know these things of myself. And now I do know of myself that they are true; for the Lord God hath made them manifest unto me by his Holy Spirit (verse 46).

So the manifestation of some fact by the Holy Spirit is, for Alma, akin to a direct perceptual experience of a fact, and notably unlike an angelic declaration of some fact.

Our formal account of belief and knowledge has helped us to recognize that belief and knowledge have something very important in common: they are both "cognitive attitudes" that is, they are in the business of mentally representing the world. Beliefs can be either true or false representations. Knowledge is a subset of belief and is always a true representation and one that is secured either directly or indirectly.

What about faith? Is faith also a type of belief?

section b: belief and faith

It is not uncommon in our everyday ways of thinking and talking to treat *faith* and *belief* as nearly synonymous. If one thinks of faith as a species of cognitive attitude, then one might suppose that there are two things that distinguish religious faith from other forms of belief. First, one might think that faith is a class of religious beliefs distinguished by what they are about, by their propositional content. Faith, you might say, involves beliefs that either directly invoke or indirectly presuppose a transcendent realm or a transcendent being. Second, one might think that faith is a class of religious beliefs distinguished by the way in which those beliefs are acquired. Faith (i.e., religious belief) cannot rest on reason and empirical evidence but ultimately must be grounded in revelation.

But the word *faith* also has a range of other meanings that can't possibly be captured by thinking of faith as a kind of belief. Faith involves something like trust or confidence as well as loyalty and commitment, fidelity and constancy, and expectancy and hope. In ordinary language, we can say, "I have faith that p"—for instance, "I have faith that Chelsea will beat Liverpool." This is a way of evaluating the truth of a proposition and saying that I believe it is true. But it also suggests that I believe it is true because I have confidence in Chelsea's abilities as a team. Interestingly enough, the Book of Mormon never uses the "faith that p" locution, although it uses "A believes that p" frequently. This suggests that the authors of the Book of Mormon didn't think of faith as a cognitive attitude.

Faith typically takes as its object, not a proposition, but a person or thing. We express this by saying, "I have faith in X"—for instance, "I have faith in Hannah." In saying that, I don't mean "I believe that Hannah speaks the truth"; I mean something more like "I have confidence in Hannah. I trust that she'll do the right thing."

In the Book of Mormon, however, faith is an attitude that always and exclusively takes as its object God and Christ.[1] No one in the Book of Mormon says things like "I have faith in Helaman." God alone is an apt object for the kind of loyalty and devotion that faith implies.

Cognitive attitudes like belief and knowledge evaluate ideas about the world by sorting them into categories of the true and the false. Faith, as it is understood in the book of Alma, also performs a kind of evaluation. But it doesn't evaluate ideas for their truth and falsity; it evaluates persons as either being worthy or unworthy of loyalty and devotion. Faith evaluates not by thinking about things or forming judgments about things but by actively responding to them. Faith, you might say, has a volitional aspect—it is concerned with our willing or resolving to act in a particular way. For example, when Moroni sees Amalickiah and his hostile armies preparing for war, Moroni begins "preparing the minds of the people to be faithful" (Alma 48:7). How does he do this? Not by preaching to them or by reasoning with them—not, that is, by providing them with proofs and arguments that might sustain them in their cognitive assent to any particular proposition. Instead, Moroni puts them to work at securing the material conditions of their religious practice. He has them "erect small forts," build "walls of stone," and in general "fortify and strengthen the land" (verses 8–9). He "prepares the minds of the people to be faithful" by getting them to actively demonstrate their trust in God. Here, the opposite of faith is not unbelief; it is the sin of inconstancy, disloyalty, or betrayal—a failure to live up to one's duties and commitments to God (Alma 44:4).

In the book of Alma, then, faith always involves "exercise"—and not just in a metaphorical sense of mental exertion. Faith simply is not faith unless it motivates bodily work and exertion and movement. To have faith is to be "faithful in keeping the commandments of God" (Alma 48:15). Attitudes that are contrary to faith, Alma suggests, include transgression, hard-heartedness, and idleness.[2]

Another aspect of the active character of faith deserves particular emphasis: faith in the book of Alma typically has an aim or a goal it is trying to achieve. For instance, in helping to explain faith to the Zoramites, Amulek emphasizes that they need to "exercise [their] faith unto repentance" (Alma 34:17). Moroni's faith aimed at maintaining a form of life centered on Christ: "this was the faith of Moroni, and his heart did glory in it; not in the shedding of blood but in doing good, in preserving his people, yea, in keeping the commandments of God, yea, and resisting iniquity" (Alma 48:16). Faith thus evaluates the world by directing us toward certain goals and away from others.

In emphasizing that Moroni's "heart did glory in [faith]," this passage also points to another important way in which faith evaluates the world: in addition to the active dimension, faith involves an affective dimension—it gives us a certain way of feeling about things. Or you might say that faith is a mood that shows us immediately what really matters in a situation. President Russell M. Nelson has emphasized the importance of this affective dimension:

> Whenever I hear anyone, including myself, say, "I know the Book of Mormon is true," I want to exclaim, "That's nice, but it is not enough!" We need to feel, deep in "the inmost part" of our hearts [Alma 13:27], that the Book of Mormon is unequivocally the word of God. We must feel it so deeply that we would never want to live even one day without it.[3]

Glorying in doing good, resoluteness, absolute trust—these are the affective components of faith in the Book of Alma. Faith evaluates the world through our feelings insofar as these feelings turn us toward some things while turning us away from others.

Faith also involves a way of looking right through present concerns to disclose the true significance of things (a significance that gets concealed by worldly preoccupations). Alma calls this "look[ing] forward with an eye of faith" (Alma 5:15). And it is a basic criterion of faith that "if ye have faith ye hope for things which are not seen, which are true" (Alma 32:21).

To sum this all up, I'd describe faith in the Book of Alma as a "practical stance." A practical stance is an evaluative attitude that differs in crucial respects from cognitive attitudes. A cognitive attitude, we said, evaluates propositions for their truth or falsity. A practical stance evaluates persons or things or deeds or the world itself, and it evaluates them in terms of the appropriate way of actively responding to them. We are constantly taking up practical stances, and most of them do not have names. When I slide behind the steering wheel of my car, I take up the practical stance of a driver. I see the dashboard and the stick shift and the road in front of me in terms of the opportunities they offer me for locomotion. If I am a good driver, I will immediately feel (without needing to think about it) when it is appropriate to use my signals, to change lanes, to speed up and slow down, and I will respond accordingly. In so doing, I will be evaluating the meaning of the things I encounter. Being able to inhabit the practical stance of a driver thus involves

    ① perceptual capacities for perceiving the features of a situation that are relevant to propelling a car through it;

    ② affective responses—feelings and moods— that guide my actions (for instance, feeling when it is necessary to shift into third gear, or to slow down in anticipation of a turn);

    ③ purposive actions, directed at the end of motoring to some destination.

Faith is understood in the Book of Alma as a practical stance. I evaluate the world in faith when I see the people and situations I encounter as God would see them, and then respond accordingly. Faith is made up of a particular readiness to act in the world, a readiness that expresses our devotion to serving God. Faith in God involves distinctive ways of seeing, feeling, and acting. For example, if I see that "a brother or sister is naked, and destitute of daily food," I might cognitively evaluate this by forming the following judgment: "They should keep warm and eat something." But if I had faith in Christ, I would evaluate this situation by ① seeing them as deserving my kindness (and in seeing them I will look right through my current worldly preoccupations, which will no longer show up as that important). I would see this immediately; I wouldn't need to think about it. My faith in Christ would also evaluate the situation by ② feeling the love of Christ for my impoverished brothers and sisters. Ultimately, a faithful way of evaluating this circumstance would involve ③ acting for a purpose ordained by God—in this case, feeding and clothing them (see James 2:15–16). Both beliefs and knowledge can contribute to the practical stance of faith in Christ (in a way yet to be determined). But if our actions have to be guided by a deliberate judgment formed on the basis of beliefs, this is a sign that our faith is immature or weak. The stronger my faith, the less I need to think about how I ought to feel and what I ought to do, and the more I will just see, feel, and act as Christ would.

Pulling it all together, I'd offer the following preliminary definition of faith as a complex evaluative attitude:

Faith is a practical stance of active loyalty to and trust in God.[4]

In describing it as a stance, I'm emphasizing that faith changes our dispositions—the way we perceive and feel about the world. In describing faith as active, I'm emphasizing that faith simply isn't faith if we are not involved in pursuing the aims and goals ordained by God.

Faith as a practical stance is thus distinctively different than belief and knowledge, which (to review) are both species of cognitive evaluations:

- Belief is an attitude in which some A holds it to be true that p.
- Knowledge is an attitude in which Ⓐ some A holds it to be true that p, Ⓑ it is true that p, and Ⓒ A's holding it to be true that p is secured in some appropriate way.

These formal definitions should make it perfectly clear just how very different faith and belief are.

section c: believing in, believing on, and knowing-how
Let's close this chapter with a quick look at other attitudes that straddle the divide between the practical and the cognitive.

In his sermon to the people of Gideon, Alma teaches that the Christ "will take upon him [his people's] infirmities, that his bowels may be filled with mercy, according to the flesh, that he may know according to the flesh how to succor his people according to their infirmities" (Alma 7:12). This intriguing idea—that God gains, through his incarnation, a kind of know-how—is discussed nowhere else in the book of Alma or, indeed, the Book of Mormon. But the type of knowledge invoked here is arguably not a propositional form of "knowing that p." When I know-how to perform some action—take, for example, knowing how to ride a bicycle—this is a practical attitude. It involves bodily skills and perceptual capacities that may depend on very little, if any, propositional knowledge. "Know-how" in general is a practical rather than a cognitive attitude, and it seems likely that Alma is attributing to the embodied Christ a kind of practical knowing that adds something new to what can be known by the spirit. "The Spirit knoweth [knows-that] all things" (Alma 7:13), but without Christ's incarnation and condescension it apparently doesn't know-how to succor God's people.

The book of Alma also uses two other locutions that seem to indicate attitudes that involve both practical and cognitive aspects: "believing in" and "believing on." For instance, the narrator notes that "there were many in the church who believed in the flattering words of Amalickiah" (Alma 46:7). Nehor's followers "believed on his word" (Alma 1:7). Frequent allusion is made to "believing in the word of God" (see Alma 32:16) or "believing in traditions" (see Alma 3:8, 11; 8:11). These are hybrid attitudes. They involve a cognitive assessment—accepting certain propositions as true (the propositions handed down by the fathers, or propositions contained in the teachings of Abinadi or Alma or Amalickiah, or the propositions of Nehor or of the scriptures). But they also involve a practical stance of trust or confidence; to believe in the word of God is to commit to accept those words as authoritative when deciding how to act.

Thus, I can believe something without believing on it, because *believing on* involves a kind of active reliance on what I believe. Believing on someone's words goes beyond merely accepting that some proposition is true; it also involves guiding my actions in accordance with that person's words. This distinction will prove to be very important to understanding Alma's Sermon on the Seed, which we will discuss in chapter 4.

2

Alma and Korihor

The young Alma and the apostate Korihor are strikingly similar—in fact, they are practically mirror images of each other. Alma "led [many] away unto destruction" (Alma 36:14) by "speak[ing] much flattery to the people" (Mosiah 27:8). Korihor was "the means of bringing many souls down to destruction, by...[his] flattering words" (Alma 30:47). Korihor demanded: "show me a sign, that I may be convinced that there is a God, yea, show unto me that he hath power" (Alma 30:43). Alma was visited by an angel "to convince [him] of the power and authority of God" (Mosiah 27:14). Alma "became dumb, that he could not open his mouth" (Mosiah 27:19). Korihor, too, "was struck dumb, that he could not have utterance" (Alma 30:50). Korihor concluded: "I know that nothing save it were the power of God could bring this upon me" (Alma 30:52). Alma, similarly, "knew that there was nothing save the power of God" that could explain what he experienced (Mosiah 27:18).

All these similarities make the points of contrast so much more striking. In response to his dramatic encounter with the power of God, Alma experienced a sudden change in his "practical stance." This involved a change in the way he perceived the world, and in his emotional response to the deeds and situations he witnessed. For instance, looking back at his past activities he was now "racked with torment" and "harrowed up by the memory of [his] many sins" (Alma 36:17). His changed practical stance was also evident in the way he was disposed, from that time forward, to respond to the people around him:

"from that time even until now," he explained later to his son Helaman, "I have labored without ceasing, that I might bring souls unto repentance; that I might bring them to taste of the exceeding joy of which I did taste" (verse 24).

For Korihor, by contrast, the changes that resulted from his experience of God's power were entirely cognitive: "Korihor put forth his hand and wrote, saying: I *know that* I am dumb, for I cannot speak; and I *know that* nothing save it were the power of God could bring this upon me" (Alma 30:52; emphasis supplied). One looks in vain to find in Korihor a repentant change of heart or a desire to reclaim the souls of those he led astray.

Despite all the similarities in their initial character traits and practices, then, Alma and Korihor couldn't be more different in the way they responded to the dramatic signs that each received. And the difference comes down to this: Alma responded in faith, while Korihor responded intellectually.

As I did with the argument in the previous chapter, I will formalize Korihor's argument to exhibit clearly its logical structure. With Korihor, this is very easy to do! He presents his message as a valid rational argument of the sort one might expect from a philosopher, and I can restate the argument in logical form with only the very slightest of modifications. But a valid argument is not the same thing as a good or a sound argument. An argument is valid when its conclusions follow from its premises. An argument is good when it is valid and its premises are true. If we lay the argument out formally, it will be easier to identify which of Korihor's premises are false.

The following is Korihor's most basic principle:
(1) *If you do not see X, then you cannot know of X* (Alma 30:15).
I'll call this Korihor's "skeptical principle." As we saw in chapter 1, it was common in Nephite culture of the time to ground knowledge in direct perceptual experience.

Korihor merely elevated a common prejudice to a strict principle. Many unwary Nephites would have accepted the skeptical principle without much question.

Korihor also assumed the following premise (although he never explicitly stated it):

② *You cannot see things in the future.*

All of Korihor's arguments are rigorously and logically derived from ① and ② together. For instance, they together entail another one of Korihor's central teachings about knowledge:

③ *If X is in the future, then you cannot know of X* (verse 13).

From principle ③, it's simple to see why Korihor is "Anti-Christ":

> He was Anti-Christ, for he began to preach unto the people against the prophecies which had been spoken by the prophets, concerning the coming of Christ (verse 6).

The doctrine of the coming of Christ, Korihor reasons, teaches that we can know a future event—namely that

④ *Christ will come in the future.*

But ③ and ④ together entail that

⑤ *you cannot know of Christ.*

The doctrine of the coming of Christ as taught by Alma also holds that the atonement and the remission of sins are future events. Alma himself, in a sermon to the people of Gideon years earlier, had said:

> I trust that…ye do worship the true and the living God, and that ye look forward for the remission of your sins, with an everlasting faith, which is to come (Alma 7:6).

In constructing his argument, Korihor actually appears to quote Alma's sermon in support of his argument. Korihor says:

> Ye look forward and say that ye see a remission of your sins. But behold, it is the effect of

a frenzied mind; and this derangement of your minds comes because of the traditions of your fathers, which lead you away into a belief of things which are not so. And many more such things did he say unto them, telling them that there could be no atonement made for the sins of men. (30:16–17)

Notice here how Korihor diagnoses what he takes to be the reason for the error of the followers of Christ: the traditions of their fathers cause them to have a "derangement of mind"—that is, a disorder or incapacity in their powers of intellect. The traditional teachings of the church of God, Korihor claims, lead to a kind of madness in which emotional agitation overwhelms a people's ability to reason properly. Their impaired cognitive capacities lead them "into a belief of things which are not so."

Quite apart from the question of whether this is an accurate diagnosis, it is not without justification that Korihor concludes that the doctrine of Christ's coming is committed to the following premise:

⑥ *When Christ comes in the future, he will atone for and remit our sins.*

But together premise ⑥ and premise ③ entail that

⑦ *You cannot know that there will be an atonement and a remission of sins.*

Up until this point, Korihor assumes only premises ① and ②. He borrows premises ④ and ⑥ from Alma's teachings. Everything else follows logically from those premises. Premise ③ follows validly from ① and ②. Premise ⑤ follows validly from ③ and ④. Premise ⑦ follows validly from ③ and ⑥. So if premises ① and ② are true, then Korihor has presented a good argument to the effect that we cannot know of Christ, of the atonement, or of a remission of sins.

Alma offers two basic types of response to Korihor's assault on the church. The most important way that

Alma responds is through an indirect attack on Korihor's background assumption that rational arguments should be decisive when it comes to matters of faith. We've seen in chapter 1 that Alma understands faith and belief to operate in different domains. Faith is a practical stance; it involves trust even in the face of doubt and consists in having one's dispositions-to-act attuned to Christ. Belief and knowledge, by contrast, are cognitive attitudes that are only indirectly related to faith. We'll look more closely in chapter 4 at Alma's indirect response to skepticism about Christ.

In the remainder of this chapter, however, I want to review Alma's second type of response to Korihor. This type of response consists in taking on the argument in its own terms. As we'll see, Alma succeeds in calling into doubt Korihor's fundamental skeptical principle—premise ①. Alma begins, however, by highlighting just how limited Korihor's conclusions are.

Even if Korihor's skeptical principle were correct, it would entitle him to conclude at most, as he does in ⑦, that you cannot know that there will be an atonement and remission of sins. But Korihor proceeds to make a stronger claim than this:

⑧ *There cannot be an atonement.* (Alma 30:17)

However, premise ⑧ does not follow from ③ and ⑥. This is like arguing that because I cannot know it will rain in Costa Mesa on July 31, 2046, it therefore cannot rain in Costa Mesa on that date. So concluding premise ⑧ on the basis of ③ and ⑥ is an error in reasoning. Likewise, Korihor oversteps what his principle entitles him to claim about God's existence. From the premise that

⑨ *God "never has been seen,"* (Alma 30:28)

Korihor concludes that

⑩ *"God . . . never was nor ever will be"* (verse 28)— *that is God never did and never will exist.*

But combining premises ① and ⑨ only entitles him to a more modest conclusion:

⑪ *You cannot know of God.*

In other words, if he were being strictly consistent, Korihor would conclude only that we lack absolute surety that there is a God. But of course one can consistently believe that there is a God (or, better, have faith in God), even while acknowledging that one doesn't know that there is a God.

So Korihor is himself guilty of leading his followers "away into a belief of things which are not so"—namely, by convincing them to believe that he has proven that there is no God, no Christ, no atonement, and no remission of sins. Alma calls him on this logical error:

> And now what evidence have ye that there is
> no God, or that Christ cometh not? I say unto
> you that ye have none, save it be your word only.
> (verse 40)

After some back and forth, Korihor wisely backs off to the more defensible position of premise ⑪ and concedes:

> I do not deny the existence of a God, but I do not
> believe that there is a God; and I say also, that ye
> do not know that there is a God. (verse 48)

Korihor's skeptical principle forbids him from claiming knowledge when he lacks a direct personal experience with the things of which he speaks. But denying that God exists amounts to claiming knowledge about God (albeit knowledge that there is no God). And so Alma forces Korihor to fall back on the more modest claim that one can know neither that God exists nor that God doesn't exist.

Alma's other direct response to Korihor undermines Korihor's skeptical principle. Remember that Korihor's entire argument hangs on the premise that

① *If you do not see X, then you cannot know of X.*

To undermine this premise, all Alma has to do is show that there are ways to arrive at a knowledge of X other than through direct perceptual experience. If Alma can show that perception is not the only means of securing knowledge, then Korihor's argument will fall apart. This is what Alma does when he asserts the following:

> I say unto you, I know there is a God, and also that Christ shall come. . . . [B]ehold, I have all things as a testimony that these things are true; and ye also have all things as a testimony unto you that they are true. (verses 39, 41)

Alma argues, in other words, that knowledge can be secured not just by direct perceptual experience but also by the testimony or witness of some other thing. Alma goes on to list the things that he believes provide a sufficient witness to secure his assent to the proposition that there is a God and that Christ will come. The list includes

- the testimony or witness of others, including the holy prophets, who claim direct experience of God;
- the witness of the scriptures; and
- the "regular form" of the earth, of "all things that are upon the face of it," of "the planets," and of their "motion" (verse 44).

Now, for Alma's immediate purposes, it doesn't matter whether the testimony of such things is sufficient to persuade anyone to believe in God. There is a long history of arguing over whether God's existence can be proven on the basis of the harmonious design of the universe or on the testimony of others. It is interesting and significant that Alma himself never explicitly develops such an argument; this lack of argument suggests to me that Alma is not particularly interested in offering an intellectual proof of God's existence. When Alma rebukes Korihor with the observation that "thou hast had signs enough" (verse 44), I don't think he means that the evidence available to Korihor is sufficient to convince a neutral observer that there is a God. Rather, as he puts it in his later sermon to the Zoramites, the evidence is sufficient to motivate a person to "exercise a particle of faith" (Alma 32:27).

In any event, in the context of dealing with Korihor, the only thing that matters is for Alma to establish the following as a principle:

⑫ *You can know X on the basis of the testimony of Y.*

If premise ⑫ is true, then ① is false. *Testimony* is here used quite broadly to mean something like "evidence that establishes a fact." For instance, when Alma claims that "all things denote there is a God" (Alma 30:44), he's tacitly invoking ⑫—after all, to say that "*Y* denotes *X*" is to say that "*Y* is a visible sign of *X*," and thus that *Y* establishes the existence of *X* as a fact. Tellingly, Korihor accepts ⑫ when he responds:

> If thou wilt, show me a sign that I may be convinced that there is a God. Yea, show unto me that he hath power, and then will I be convinced of the truth of thy words. (verse 43)[1]

A sign is something that can be seen that indicates the existence of something else that is not seen. In accepting that a sign would convince him that there is a God, Korihor has abandoned premise ①. And with that, his entire chain of logical reasoning falls apart. The rest of the story—his receiving the sign of power and being struck dumb, his being convinced that there is a God—is epilogue.

So what are we supposed to learn from the comparison and contrast between Korihor and Alma? Here's my suggestion: when Alma received a sign—when he was confronted by the angel—this sign did of course provide intellectually cognizable evidence for the existence of God. But that was not the most important significance of the sign. The primary effect of the sign was found in its impact on his heart, not his mind. It awakens Alma to an immediate and overpowering conviction of his wrong deeds. Alma experiences his mistakes not as error in reasoning but as sin—that is, as error in his practices. This experience gives rise to intense suffering that, in turn, leads him to call upon God for a remission of sins (Alma 36:18).

When Korihor receives a sign, the principal effect the sign has on him is that it forces him to acknowledge a cognitive error: "the devil hath deceived me. . . . And he said unto me: There is no God. . . . And I have taught his words; and I taught them because they were pleasing unto the carnal *mind*" (Alma 30:53; emphasis supplied). But there is on Korihor's part no pain and suffering as a result of the harm he caused to other people. He doesn't feel guilty, and he doesn't ask for forgiveness.[2] So even if his cognitive commitments have been changed,[3] his practical stance hasn't been changed at all by the experience: "If this curse should be taken from thee," Alma observes, "thou wouldst again lead away the hearts of this people" (verse 55).

In the end, then, there is one feature of Korihor that reveals more about him than any of his arguments: his conviction that "every man prosper[s] according to his genius" (verse 17). *Genius* here means "the peculiar structure of mind which is given by nature to an individual," one's "strength of mind," one's "mental powers or faculties."[4] So the conviction that organizes Korihor's life is this: It is in virtue of our rationality and intellectual rigor that we prosper. What is Alma's view? Prospering has nothing to do with what we think or believe and everything to do with our practical stance: "Give ear to my words; for I swear unto you, that inasmuch as ye shall keep the commandments of God ye shall prosper."[5]

3

Alma among the Zoramites

Religious life involves both what we have been calling cognitive and practical attitudes. We moderns tend to emphasize the cognitive dimension in our thought and talk about faith. One important way in which we introduce children and converts to a religion is by teaching them to accept the doctrines of the church. Doctrinal disagreements are all too often the primary source of animosity and strife between competing religious sects. When we try to explain what it means to belong to a religious community, we usually fall back on a description of the doctrines to which members of the community readily assent. This is easier than trying to make explicit the differences in the active stances people take as a result of their faith.

But it would be a mistake to conclude that the cognitive dimension of religious life is more important or more fundamental than the practical dimensions of religious life. As we will see in this chapter and the next, there is a complex interrelationship between what we hold to be true and how we are poised and ready to respond practically to the world.

Consider, for example, Alma's mission to the Zoramites. Alma had received news that Zoram was leading his people to "pervert the ways of the Lord" (Alma 31:1). "Walking in the ways of the Lord" is an expression typically used in the scriptures to describe what I've been calling a practical stance centered on active devotion to the Lord. One "walks in the ways of the Lord" when one "observe[s] to keep his commandments and his statutes" (Alma 25:14). Even though the Zoramites "had had the word of God preached unto them" (Alma 31:8), they had fallen into "great errors" of a practical kind, "for they would not observe to keep the commandments of God, and his statutes, according to the law of Moses. Neither would they observe the performances of the church" (verses 9–10). It is concern over the practical apostasy of the Zoramites that initially motivates Alma to set out for Antionum (the land where the Zoramites had gathered). Alma hopes to correct the practical apostasy by teaching correct doctrine because "the preaching of the word had a great tendency to lead the people to do that which was just" (verse 5).

These passages thus suggest an intimate interconnection between one's beliefs and one's practical stance of faithfulness. The central aim of the next chapter will be to explore Alma's account of the proper relationship between belief, knowledge, and faith. But to set up that discussion, I want to focus in this chapter on Alma's diagnosis of the nature of the Zoramite apostasy. We'll look first, in section A, at Zoramite beliefs. In section B, we'll consider Alma's response to Zoramite religious practice.

section a: zoramite theology

When Alma and his companions arrived in Antionum they discovered that Zoramite worship consisted entirely in select[1] members of the community taking turns ascending a stand and offering the "selfsame prayer" (Alma 31:22) on "one day of the week" (verse 12). There are two principle parts to the Zoramites' prayer. The first part of the prayer is a catalog of beliefs that the Zoramites hold—by my count, seven of them—about God and about their relationship to God. The second part of the prayer is an expression of gratitude for the relationship to God that was described in the first part. Nowhere in the prayer, and thus nowhere in the Zoramite worship service, is any mention made of the practical obligations of membership in the church. The Zoramites apparently have no religious duties, other than perhaps to publicly declare their belief in the teachings of their church.

The Zoramites' beliefs, restated somewhat, include three claims about God's character:

① An affirmation of God's existence: "Holy, holy God; we believe that thou art God." (verse 15)

② An affirmation of God's moral and spiritual perfection: "We believe that thou art holy." (verse 15)

③ An affirmation of God's unchanging nature: "[We believe] that thou wast a spirit, and that thou art a spirit, and that thou wilt be a spirit forever." (verse 15)

Their catalog of beliefs also include four claims about the Zoramites' relationship to God:

④ Sectarianism: an affirmation that God directed them to break away from the church of God: "Holy God, we believe that thou hast separated us from our brethren." (verse 16)

⑤ Election to virtue: an affirmation that they had been chosen by God to receive moral and spiritual virtues: "We do not believe in the tradition of our brethren, which was handed down to them by the childishness of their fathers, but we believe that thou hast elected us to be thy holy children" (verse 16).

⑥ Rejection of the doctrine of the coming of Christ: a denial that a savior is needed or even possible: "Thou [God] hast made it known unto us that there shall be no Christ, but thou art the same yesterday, today, and forever" (verses 16–17).

⑦ Election to salvation: an affirmation that they had been chosen by God to receive salvation:

"[We believe] thou hast elected us that we shall be saved, whilst all around us are elected to be cast by thy wrath down to hell." (verse 17)

Belief claims ⑤ and ⑥ have a grammatical form that merits some attention. Each contains two independent clauses connected by the conjunction *but*. The first clause makes a negative claim—in these cases, asserting that something is not believed or known—followed by a positive claim that makes a positive assertion. The important thing to recognize is that the second, positive clause explains and justifies the first, negative clause. For example, in belief claim ⑤ it is not the case that the Zoramites simply have stopped believing in the religious traditions practiced by the Nephites. They've stopped believing in these traditions *because* they believe that they have been elected—that is, selected and chosen by God—to possess moral and spiritual virtues. The Zoramites don't need to concern themselves with religious practices and observances, in other words, because they believe they have already found favor with God. This is the belief that explains a particular Zoramite behavior that Alma finds so peculiar: offering this prayer was, in fact, the entirety of the Zoramite religious practice: "After the people had all offered up thanks after this manner, they returned to their homes, never speaking of their God again until they had assembled themselves together again to the holy stand" (verse 23). This is indeed a peculiar practice if one believes "that ye should work out your salvation with fear before God" (Alma 34:37). But if one believes that one is already selected by God and in possession of the moral and spiritual virtues needed for salvation, then any further worship practices are superfluous.

What about Zoramite belief ⑥?

⑥ Thou hast made it known unto us that [negative claim:] there shall be no Christ, but [positive claim:] thou art the same yesterday, today, and forever.

I should note that the modern division of the Book of Mormon into verses has separated the two clauses of this sentence into different verses. This division was not in the original 1830 version of the Book of Mormon. The modern versification obscures the fact that the clause following the *but* is offered as an elucidation of the previous clause. By reuniting the divided clauses, we discover another key aspect of Zoramite religious beliefs: the Zoramites think that they can know that there shall be no Christ *because* they are certain that God is the same yesterday, today, and forever—in other words, belief ③. Belief ③—that God will be the same throughout time—is their justification for, and the explanation of, their confident assertion that ⑥ no savior is needed or even possible.

This assertion—and, indeed, the prayer as a whole, with its heavy emphasis on belief—reveals a great deal about the importance of cognition to Zoramite religion. The Zoramites' rejection of the doctrine of the coming of Christ follows rationally from their beliefs about the unchanging nature of God. Thus, where Korihor (when consistent) argued for the weaker conclusion—that he couldn't know either that there will or will not be a Christ—the Zoramites make the stronger argument: they can affirmatively know that there will not be a Christ. They know this, they reasoned, because God's incarnation would represent a change in the unchanging character of God.

Another indication of the importance of belief and knowledge to the Zoramite religion is found in the way the Zoramites connect election and wealth. Alma suggests that the Zoramites inferred that they were God's elect because they were wealthy (Alma 31:28). And the Zoramite priests seem to have drawn the complementary inference that the poor were not among God's elect because they were poor: "[We] are despised of all men because of [our] poverty," the foremost of the poor Zoramites notes, "and more especially by our priests; for they have cast us out of our synagogues" (Alma 32:5). The poor are "not permitted to enter into their synagogues to worship God, being esteemed as filthiness" (verse 3), because the worship would involve these poor people asserting their election to virtue—a condition that (in the minds of the Zoramites) is clearly belied by their poverty.

section b: Alma's response

When Alma observes the Zoramite prayer, he discovers that the Zoramites are directly attacking the teachings of the church of God, and the doctrine of the coming of Christ in particular, on rationalist grounds. But what Alma most immediately reacts to is not what the Zoramites believe. It's what their form of worship reveals about their practical stance—about what they do, how they feel, and how they perceive the world around them:

> Now when Alma saw this his heart was grieved; for he saw that they were a wicked and a perverse people; yea, he saw that their hearts were set upon gold, and upon silver, and upon all manner of fine goods. Yea, and he also saw that their hearts were lifted up unto great boasting, in their pride. (Alma 31:24–25)

Years later, in his advice to his son Corianton, Alma singles out the Zoramites' practical stance as the greatest flaw in their worship practices: "Do not pray as the Zoramites do," Alma explains, "for ye have seen that they pray to be heard of men, and to be praised for their wisdom" (Alma 38:13). No mention is made of the Zoramites' apostate beliefs.

When beliefs are mistaken, the result is "error." When faith is mistaken, it is a "perversion" of the ways of the Lord. *Perversion* in the context of the Book of Mormon does not have the sexual connotations that it does in modern English usage. "To pervert" comes from the Latin *pervertare*, meaning "to turn something the wrong way." A practice is perverted when it is distorted or corrupted so that it no longer serves its proper purpose. Alma's primary objection to the Zoramites is their perversion of the life of faith. They have turned the practical stance of faith in God upside down and have distorted it into an excuse for pride and greed rather than a call to love and mercy.

The Zoramites' errors, their mistaken beliefs, are of concern only to the extent that these mistaken beliefs prove an obstacle to developing the right practical stance. Alma singles out two Zoramite beliefs as deserving a response: ⑥ the rejection of Christ's coming, and ⑦ the belief in election to salvation. Alma suggests that both of these doctrines encourage an attitude of materialistic pride (see Alma 31:27–29).

Because Alma mentions the Zoramites' doctrines only to decry their prideful and materialistic practical stance, the implication is that Alma's principal objection to these doctrines is their effect on the Zoramites' practical stance. We'll see in the next chapter that Alma regards a feeling or mood of humility as fundamental to a practical stance of faith. Thus, to the extent that the Zoramites believe they are already elect and do not need a savior, their cognitive attitudes are an obstacle to faith.

Alma's understanding of the proper relationship between belief and faith is perhaps most clearly revealed in the way that he responds to these beliefs. Alma embarked on his mission, after all, with the express purpose of "preaching the word" to the Zoramites. And one might thus expect him to offer reasons and mount an argument to try to persuade the Zoramites directly that their beliefs are false. This is precisely what Alma doesn't do. He doesn't engage in a theological reflection on the nature of God's sameness through time. Those who have an intellectual bent may find this to be a genuinely interesting theological problem: How could God be the same yesterday, today, and forever, while also changing in significant respects (like living a mortal existence, being born of a woman, suffering, and dying)? But these are doctrinal concerns that Alma never takes up.

Instead, Alma's approach is indirect. Rather than responding with a direct appeal to the mind, Alma works to plant the word in the Zoramites' hearts. And he does this only when the Zoramites come to him, not with an intellectual question but with an eminently practical question: "Behold, what shall we do?" (Alma 32:5).

> And now when Alma heard this, he turned him about, his face immediately towards him, and he beheld with great joy; for he beheld that their afflictions had truly humbled them, and that *they were in a preparation to hear the word.* (verse 6, emphasis supplied)

4

Faith as a Practical Stance

Alma's Sermon on the Seed (contained in Alma 32 and 33) is perhaps one of the best-loved passages in the Book of Mormon. Primary children sing about it. Missionaries introduce investigators to it early on in the missionary discussions. The imagery used in the sermon—seeds, trees, ground, and fruits—makes it readily accessible even to those who are young in the faith. And Alma develops in the sermon a powerful account of the relationship between faith and knowledge that will interest anyone with a serious concern for religious life.

But to fully appreciate the Sermon on the Seed, readers must see it in the larger context of Alma's efforts to respond to Zoramite attacks on his faith and religious practices. This context is easy to miss, given that Alma does not directly address the arguments, reasons, and evidence in favor of his beliefs, or against the Zoramite creed. Of the seven core beliefs of the Zoramites, Alma's sermon touches on only one of them—the rejection of the doctrine of Christ's coming. Even so, Alma never presents an argument directly targeting the Zoramite argument that there can be no Christ. Alma offers his audience nothing in the way of theological arguments because his target is not their minds—their cognitive attitudes. His target is their hearts and their practical stance of faith: "I desire that ye shall plant this word in your hearts, and as it beginneth to swell even so nourish it by your faith (Alma 33:23). By targeting the heart, Alma calls into question the idea that our cognitive attitudes are decisive when it comes to matters of faith.

This sermon thus amounts to an indirect attack on the Zoramite emphasis on correct belief.

Alma's indirect response aims at changing our assumptions about the proper relationship between faith and mental attitudes like belief and knowledge. These assumptions, by and large, operate in the background. If we are raised to assume that faith is a kind of belief, we may think that we're supposed to discover a secure rational foundation for our faith. But if faith is a practical stance rather than a cognitive attitude, it's not the kind of thing that needs rational foundations. A practical stance has its own type of surety—not the surety of intellectual justification but the conviction that comes from successfully achieving one's aims and coping with challenges. The practical stance of a bike rider, for instance, is not secured by a cognitive understanding of the physics involved in staying upright on a moving bicycle. If you ask an experienced bike rider to prove that her bike-riding practical stance is correct, she doesn't give you an argument; she gets on her bike and rides it. Her practical stance is "confirmed" when the rider reliably propels her bicycle over a variety of roads and fluidly negotiates a variety of obstacles to successfully reach her destination. Likewise, it would be (at best) a distraction for beginning riders to worry about the theoretical foundations of bike physics. A rational understanding contributes almost nothing to developing the skills one needs to learn to ride a bike.

So if Alma can change our background assumptions about the "proof" that is appropriate to faith, this will create a space for developing new practices and skills for responding to the world—practices and skills centered on trust in Christ. The exercise of those practices, in turn, changes the way people experience the world. Alma promises that our new practical stance will eventually have its confirmation when we reliably negotiate the challenges of human existence. If received, this confirmation should be more than enough to satisfy any reasonable set of demands for justification of faith.

Alma's Sermon on the Seed shows us how to shift our background assumptions about faith. I'll review Alma's account in three stages. In section A, we'll review Alma's distinction between the mind and the heart. We'll then, in Section B, look in some detail at the Sermon on the Seed. In section C, we'll explore the implications of the sermon for a true understanding of the relationship between knowledge and faith. We'll conclude in section D with some observations about the role that joy plays in confirming the heart's judgment.

section a: minds and hearts

How are we to understand the contrast between the heart and the mind? In the book of Alma, the mind is the faculty responsible for belief (and unbelief; see Alma 19:6; 30:16). Our ability to understand thoughts and doctrines is located in the mind (see Alma 36:18; 39:16), as is our capacity for questioning or inquiring (see Alma 34:5) or remembering (see Alma 13:1). The mind decides upon a course of deliberate action (see Alma 2:5; 17:6). The mind is disabled by blindness—an inability to discern the truth (see Alma 14:6). When Alma refers to a person's mind, then, he is talking about that person's cognitive attitudes and capacities.

The heart, by contrast, is the faculty of feelings like joy (see Alma 17:29; 19:13; 22:8; 26:11), anger (see Alma 27:12), or depression (see Alma 26:27). The heart is also the seat of our dispositions, or what we might call character traits or temperaments—things like pride or humility (see Alma 5:53; 6:3; 32:3–4), courage (see Alma 15:4; 62:1), stubbornness (see Alma 32:16), or gratitude (see Alma 37:37; 48:12). The heart contains our wishes and desires (see 19:33; 29:1; 39:11), and affections (see Alma 13:29; 37:36). The heart is also the source of our intentions (see Alma 11:25; 18:32; 47:4)—suggesting that it is ultimately our desires, feelings, and dispositions rather than our rational deliberations that move us to act. Whereas the mind is disabled by blindness, the heart is disabled by hardness—a fixity of character, feeling, or purpose. The person who is hard of heart is unable to flexibly respond to the enticings of the spirit or to changing circumstances. In the book of Alma, talking about a person's heart is shorthand for that person's "practical stance"—the agent's readiness to act for some purpose, as guided by his or her dispositions and emotions.

With the distinction between mind and heart in place,[1] we can see that Alma's goal in the Sermon on the Seed is to persuade people that acceptance of the doctrine of the coming of Christ is first and foremost a matter for the heart, and only subsequently a matter for the mind. This will undoubtedly strike many as a dubious proposal, given that the mind is the faculty tasked with understanding and evaluating doctrines. But Alma gives us detailed instructions in the Sermon on the Seed on how we can take the doctrine of the coming of Christ into our hearts and live it, rather than merely believe it. So, stripped to its essentials, the meaning of the Sermon on the Seed is this: faith in Christ is not a cognitive evaluation of the doctrines or teaching about Christ; it is a practical evaluation of the world in the light of Christ.

section b: the sermon on the seed
Popular accounts of the sermon often get it wrong in their telling of the details of the sermon's central

metaphor—the planting, sprouting, and eventual fruition of the seed. At the risk of disappointing Primary children all around the world, I note that in Alma's telling, faith is not "like a little seed...swelling within my heart."[2] Rather, the *word* is like a seed: "We will compare the word unto a seed" (Alma 32:28). When the seed begins to grow, its growth shows "that this is a good seed, or that the word is good, for it beginneth to enlarge my soul; yea, it beginneth to enlighten my understanding, yea, it beginneth to be delicious to me" (verse 28). This is not a claim about faith getting stronger—that will happen too, but as a side effect of the principal change that the word causes in my heart: "Now behold, would not this [that is, the growing of the seed] increase your faith? I say unto you, Yea" (verse 29). So the increase in faith accompanies the growing of the seed but is not identical to it. The close connection between the growing of the seed and the increase in faith is undoubtedly part of the reason why faith is so routinely confused with the seed. But—and here is the danger of misstating the metaphorical meaning—the aim of planting the seed in your heart is not that your faith can grow into knowledge. Alma is only peripherally interested in the knowledge (such as it is) that accompanies the growth of the seed (see section C). The fruit of the seed then is not knowledge; it is a joyful harmony with all good things in the world (see section D). This harmony grows as devotion to God transforms one's heart ("enlarges my soul"), expands one's mind ("enlightens my understanding"), and changes one's tastes ("begins to be delicious to me").

If faith is not the seed, then what is the metaphor for faith? Faith is what you "exercise" to plant the seed (Alma 32:27; 34:4). Active faith "nourish[es] the word" (Alma 32:41–42; 33:23). Thus, the metaphor for faith is a fertile and well-watered soil that nourishes and sustains the seed in its growth. Conversely, a lack of faith means a lack of nourishment—that is, "your ground is barren" (Alma 32:39).

The seed thus represents not faith but the proper object of faith. As we have noted, faith is an attitude that involves some object (a person or a thing) in which one trusts, and to whom one pledges one's loyalty. The seed planted in the heart is a metaphorical description of an attitude of trust or loyalty directed at the proper object of faith. But we have also noted already that God is always the proper object of faith in the Book of Mormon. Why, then, does Alma say the seed is the word? The word is the "word of God" or, perhaps more precisely, the seed is God as understood according to a particular doctrinal teaching. Alma concludes the sermon by spelling out this teaching:

> the Son of God...will come to redeem his people, and...he shall suffer and die to atone for their sins; and...he shall rise again from the dead, which shall bring to pass the resurrection, that all men shall stand before him, to be judged at the last and judgment day, according to their works. And now, my brethren, *I desire that ye shall plant this word in your hearts* (Alma 33:22–23; emphasis supplied).

On Alma's understanding of faith as a practical stance, then, the first necessary condition of a genuine faith is that one is loyal to and trusts in the Son of God who will come into the world, suffer and die to redeem his people, be resurrected, and judge everyone according to their works (verse 22). These doctrinal claims direct us to a God whose primary attributes are justice and mercy, a God who can be trusted both to set the world right and to succor his people. (See chapter 7 for a more detailed discussion of God's character according to Alma.)

The Sermon on the Seed describes a reciprocal interaction between the seed—the word of God—and the faith or practical stance that nourishes the seed and allows it to grow. As our faithful stance nurtures the seed, the seed grows—that is, our understanding of God improves. To understand God better, we have to be more like him. We "receive his image in our countenances" (Alma 5:14). As the seed swells and grows, our faith increases—that is, we become better at actively serving God. Our practical stance becomes purer, more skillful, more immediately responsive to the needs of those around us. Let's track this process in more detail in three steps: ① receiving the word, ② growing the seed, and ③ increasing in faith.

1. receiving the word

Alma's sermon is inspired by a simple question. The foremost representative of the poorest class of the Zoramites asks Alma, "What shall we do?" (Alma 32:5). The question is motivated by the fact that this poor class of Zoramites has "no place to worship [their] God," for they "were not permitted to enter into their synagogues to worship God, being esteemed as filthiness; therefore they were poor; yea, they were esteemed by their brethren as dross" (verse 3). Alma's response to their question could have been simple and direct: he could have taught them that they don't have to worship God in any particular place. And that is exactly what Alma does—only much later in the sermon (see Alma 33:2). His immediate reply is unexpected and indirect: "It is well that ye are cast out of your synagogues" (Alma 32:12).

Why does Alma offer such a seemingly unsympathetic response? Because, for him, there is a question to answer before we ask, "What should we do to worship God?" The more important question is, "How do true worshippers of God carry themselves?" Or, to put it slightly differently, Alma's question is, "What kind of disposition sets us on the path to faith?" His answer is "humility." Alma thus "beheld with great joy" that "their afflictions had truly humbled them, and that they were in a preparation to hear the word" (Alma 32:6). Alma discerns in their plight an opportunity for the Zoramites to have their responses to the world re-attuned, and this is a vital starting point on the path to faith.

So humility is the key dispositional characteristic in the development of faith. Yet, as Alma notes, there are different kinds of humility. He distinguishes between those "who truly humble themselves" and those who "were compelled to be humble" (verse 14; see also verses 6 and 15). The latter kind of humility—a humility that involves a sense of inferiority to others, of unworthiness or even humiliation—is of no interest to Alma. But what is "true humility"? And why is true humility a necessary condition of faith?

The humble person "believeth in the word of God" and submits to the word of God "without stubbornness of heart, yea, without being brought to know the word, or even compelled to know, before they will believe [in it]" (verse 16). It is important to note that Alma here is talking about believing *in*, not believing *that*. As we saw in chapter 1, believing in the word involves accepting the word as authoritative for my actions. Humility sets us on the path to faith because true humility is the kind of submissiveness that responds to promptings without first demanding a complete satisfaction of the intellect:

> Blessed is he that believeth in the word of God . . . without stubbornness of heart. . . . Yea, there are many who do say: If thou wilt show unto us a sign from heaven, then we shall know of a surety; then we shall believe. Now I ask, is this faith? Behold, I say unto you, Nay; for

if a man knoweth a thing he hath no cause to believe [in it],[3] for he knoweth it (verses 16–18).

Two quick notes about these verses. First, the phrase "cause to believe" is a key to understanding Alma's point. In the American English of Joseph Smith's time, "the primary sense" of the word "cause" "is to urge, press, impel....A cause is...the reason or motive that urges, moves, or impels the mind to act or decide."[4] Having a cause to believe in x lies somewhere between being compelled or forced to believe in x, and merely having a reason to believe in x. If I have a cause to believe in, say, the golden rule, that means that I feel urged or impelled to take it as my guide to life. I don't just idly recognize that it might give someone a reason to act. Thus, when Alma says that "if a man knoweth a thing he hath no cause to believe in it," part of what he means is that knowledge alone is motivationally inert. I can know that something is true without being moved to take it as my guide.

Second note: when Alma asks "Is this faith?," the word *this* does not refer to "know of a surety." In other words, Alma is not asking, "Is knowledge faith?"[5] Instead, *this* here refers to the act of saying: "If you will show us a sign from heaven, then we will know of a surety, and then we will believe." If I demand to know that p is true before believing in p, that is an example of a faithless stubbornness of heart. My hardness of heart— that is, my lack of humility—consists precisely in holding out for intellectual certainty when I already have a cause to believe in the word (i.e., I already feel moved to use the word to guide my actions).

Now someone might say at this point: "It's not a bad thing to demand certainty before submitting your will to the guidance of some code of conduct. That's a good thing! It's a mark of rational agency to want to know something is true before committing oneself to follow it." Alma, however, holds that such an attitude is morally flawed. He asks:

> And now, how much more cursed is he that knoweth the will of God and doeth it not, than he that only believeth, or only hath cause to believe, and falleth into transgression? (verse 19)

Let's try to unpack this somewhat obscure passage. For starters, we can translate it into a more modern idiom. *Cursed* means "deserving of curse"—that is, "deserving of condemnation." So rather than asking, "How much more cursed is he?," we could ask, "How much more blameworthy is he?" Secondly, if something is the will of God, then obeying it is doing what is right, and transgressing it is doing what is wrong. So we can talk simply of doing right and doing wrong. In this passage, then, Alma poses this question: When a person knows what is right and doesn't do it, is he more blameworthy than a person who only believes that it is right and doesn't do it?

The following is Alma's answer:

> Behold, I say unto you, that it is on the one hand even as it is on the other; and it shall be unto every man according to his work (verse 20).

In other words, the moral status of an action does not turn on the difference between believing an act is wrong and knowing it is wrong. For instance, if I murder someone while believing it is wrong to murder someone, it is no excuse to say, "Well, I only believed it was wrong; I didn't absolutely know it was wrong." I performed the same "work" as the murderer who knows it is wrong; I murdered while holding it to be true that murder is wrong, and thus I deserve the same punishment as the knowing murderer.[6]

The comparison to moral transgression shows that there are circumstances where it is wrong to demand knowledge before acting (or refraining from acting). In moral conduct in general, you ought to do what you believe is right or what you even merely have cause to believe is right. If you demand sure knowledge before acting, you are unreasonably stubborn.

There may well be other circumstances in which such stubbornness is a virtue. We might want scientists, for instance, to hold out for a high level of certainty before they accept a theory. But ethically speaking, stubbornness is a vice. We would be in a sorry state if people refused to accept standards of ethical behavior until they knew of a surety that those standards were true.

How about in matters of faith? Is it admirable to wait until one is either "brought to know" or "compelled to know" before one commits to following God? Alma's answer is a resounding *no*. This is because, as we will soon see, I'm able to understand the word of God only when I've been transformed through the exercise of faith. Until I've developed a practical stance of faith, I'm not in a position to be convinced that there is a God. Thus, humility is a necessary condition of faith—it is the disposition that launches us on the path to faith. True humility is a ready receptivity to enticements to do good, without stubbornly holding out for indubitable evidence.

What if I don't believe in the word, or don't even have cause to believe in the word—that is, what if I don't feel moved or urged to guide my life according to the example of Christ?

We've already seen Alma's answer. Alma thinks that a humble person will be able to perform an honest "experiment upon [his] words, and exercise a particle of faith" (verse 27). The experiment consists in this: find some "portion of [the] words" of Christ and "give place" for it in your heart (verses 27–28). I take it that any portion of the doctrine of the coming of Christ will do. Remember that the heart is the faculty of feelings, of dispositions, of wishes, of desires, of affections, and of intentions to act. So I might experiment with planting a portion of this word in my heart, for example, by resolving to act as if I am going to be judged by God according to my works. Or I might merely desire to be forgiven of my wrongful acts and let myself hope that I could, someday and somehow, be forgiven. Or I might let the word act on my affections and let myself love others without reserve—without safeguarding my heart against the inevitable death of the people and relationships around me. I'm not planting the word in my mind, so for the time being it doesn't matter whether I believe these things or not. And it will take considerable humility to conduct the experiment; I have to admit that I am not in control of my fate and that I depend on others. All that Alma's test requires of us is that we be humble enough to let those ideas work on our dispositions and desires and intentions and affections.

2. growing the seed

If we are humble enough to believe in some portion of the word—that is, to take it to heart and actively use it as a guide to life—then the effects will soon be discernable. The seed will do what any good seed does: it will grow. I will feel the effects as it begins to "swell within my breast" and "enlarge my soul" (Alma 32:28). Alma sets a three-part test on what constitutes the soul-enlarging effects of a good seed:

1. "It beginneth to enlighten my understanding" (verse 28).
2. "It beginneth to be delicious to me" (verse 28).
3. It "bringeth forth unto its own likeness" (verse 31).

Each of these is correctly described as the "growth" of the word of God because each change brings with it a deeper and richer understanding of the nature of God.

The three elements of Alma's test correspond to the three aspects of a practical stance that I outlined in chapter 2. We saw that any given practical stance involves

① specific perceptual capacities, ② specific affective responses, and ③ characteristic purposes and goals. My active devotion to God increases as I receive:

    ① an enhanced ability to perceive the world;

    ② a new mood of joy or delight;
       and

    ③ a greater commitment to works of love and
    mercy.

Let's look briefly at each aspect.

① "IT BEGINNETH TO ENLIGHTEN MY UNDERSTANDING." *This is referring to the perceptual capacities of faith.*

As the seed grows, Alma explains, "your mind doth begin to expand" (Alma 32:34). This undoubtedly involves a cognitive dimension—an enlargement of our capacity to think about, reason about, and understand things that we didn't understand before: "Your understanding doth begin to be enlightened" (verse 34). Alma (and Ammon) both argue that there are things we can know only following an existential transformation—a change in the way we exist in the world (see, e.g., Alma 26:21–22; 38:6). And it follows that there is a kind of knowledge that cannot be conveyed by proof or rational demonstration. You have to live it to understand it.

The mind expansion also involves an enhancement of our perceptual capacities. The promise is that, as the word takes hold in your heart, you will see things in a new light, and new things will be "discernible" (Alma 32:35). Alma also describes this as "looking forward with an eye of faith" (verse 40; see also Alma 5:15)—looking forward suggests not letting one's sight be arrested by present concerns. If the portion of the word that I've planted in my heart is, for instance, the idea of a final judgment according to my works, I'll see myself as responsible for the way I respond to the present situation (see, e.g., Alma 5:18–19). At first, my new perceptual capacities might involve simply a heightened awareness of my own selfishness—my tendencies to act in my own personal interest at the expense of others. Eventually, if I let this way of seeing the world take hold, what will increasingly matter and become salient to me are the things that God wants me to care about and care for.

② "IT BEGINNETH TO BE DELICIOUS
TO ME." *This is referring to the affective
dispositions of the faithful.*
The changed ability to perceive things will be accompanied by a changed way of emotionally responding to the things I see. Alma gives a delightfully synesthetic description of this change: he calls it tasting this light (Alma 32:35). As the seed takes root in our heart—as we start to perceive and act in a way that is guided by the word—Alma promises that the word will "be delicious to" us (verse 28). The light that lets us see is something that we taste, and what we taste is delicious and desirable.

Why does Alma mix up sight and taste in this way? When we taste something, we experience it with a kind of visceral immediacy, unfiltered by the concepts and categories of the intellect. We rarely have words that are fine-grained enough to capture what our tongue detects and understands. Moreover, our sense of taste guides our most basic desires—it directs us in the satisfaction of our hunger and thirst. So Alma's description of the effects of planting the seed in our hearts (in other words, the effects of faithfully acting on a humble devotion to God) includes a peculiar change in our feelings that accompanies the change in our perceptual capacities. We henceforth distinguish activities in terms of how delicious, sweet, or bitter they "taste" (see Alma

32:42; 36:21; 38:8; 40:26). The person of faith guides his or her activities accordingly.

③ "EVERY SEED BRINGETH FORTH UNTO ITS OWN LIKENESS." *This is the goal of the faithful.* Faith, we have said, interprets the world purposively as either advancing us toward or blocking our path toward the end ordained by God. What, according to Alma, is the goal of faith? Alma's answer is so simple that it is easy to miss: faith nurtures the seed, and "every seed bringeth forth unto its own likeness" (Alma 32:31). The word *unto* expresses the change of the character of the person who has planted the seed.[7] A *likeness* is something that copies or resembles another thing. So Alma's ultimate test to tell whether a seed is good is this: Does the seed produce something with a character, nature, or quality that resembles the word itself?

So as the seed grows, we'll understand God better because we will be more like him. And as we develop our faith, we will be disposed to act in the way that Christ would act. We resemble the Son of God insofar as we are able to pursue the aims and ends that Christ himself has pursued. The purposive goal of Christian faith is to produce people who take as their own aim the work of the Father—the redemptive work of succoring and showing mercy to others. (We'll return to this topic in chapter 7).

3. increasing in faith

In chapter 1, I offered the following definition of faith as it is understood in the book of Alma: *Faith is a practical stance of active loyalty to and trust in God.*

In describing faith as a stance, I emphasized how acquiring it changes our dispositions. The faithful perceive the world differently than those without faith. They feel differently about the situations they encounter. In describing faith as active, I emphasized that faith isn't faith if we are not involved in an ongoing effort to achieve the aims and goals ordained by God.

We've seen now how Alma's sermon presupposes this view of faith as a practical stance. We've seen that the proper object of faith as Alma understands it is the Son of God. The characteristic disposition of faith is humility—a receptivity to goodness in the world. This disposition brings with it an eye that looks forward and thus sees things in terms of their significance for our ultimate hope of redemption. The disposition of humility grows into a changed emotional response to the world, so that we experience as "sweet" or "delicious" the works of goodness, and as "bitter" anything that is selfish or hurtful to others. The disposition of humility aims to make us, like Christ himself, participants in the work of redemption. Faith as a practical stance is poised to respond in a Christlike way to the situations we encounter. Faith always involves an exercise.

In the context of the seed allegory, exercise or action is the soil that nourishes the word. In other words, it is not enough to imagine that some portion of the word is true; it is essential to act on the supposition that it is. Amulek identifies several aspects of the exercise that characterizes a faithful practical stance. These aspects include repentance and prayer "for the welfare of those who are around you" (Alma 34:27). But prayer alone is not active enough:

> And now behold, my beloved brethren, I say unto you, do not suppose that this is all; for after ye have done all these things, if ye turn away the needy, and the naked, and visit not the sick and afflicted, and impart of your substance, if ye have, to those who stand in need—I say unto you, if ye do not any of

these things, behold, your prayer is vain, and
availeth you nothing, and ye are as hypocrites
who do deny the faith. (verse 28)

As we are guided by the word, our hearts will be changed
in good ways, and this in and of itself will give us confidence that the word is good. As our hearts change, we
will also become more skillful at exercising our faith.
In other words, our faith will grow.

section c: faith and knowledge

By now it is clear, I hope, why the familiar, everyday
way of treating faith as a type of belief fails to capture
the full complexity of faith. While faith might involve
beliefs, it is not a cognitive attitude. It evaluates the
world, not propositions about the world. It evaluates
in the way it sees what is important and needs to be
done, in the way it feels about the people and events it
encounters, in the way it acts in situations, and in the
purposes it aims to achieve. Thus, when Alma insists
that "faith is not to have a perfect knowledge of things"
(Alma 32:21), this should not be heard as a criticism
of faith—as if faith is a flawed, inferior version of the
kind of attitude that knowledge is. This should rather
be heard as Alma saying that faith and knowledge are
fundamentally different types of attitudes and belong
in different categories.

One way to recognize this distinction is to note that
Alma thinks that knowledge is in the service of faith
rather than the other way around. As the seed starts
to swell and grow, this will give us the direct experi-
ential surety that allows us to conclude that "this is
a good seed." The result is not to replace faith with
knowledge. Rather, "it will strengthen your faith: for
ye will say 'I know that this is a good seed'" (verse 30).
There may even be cases in which your knowledge is
perfect in some thing and your faith is momentarily

"dormant" (verse 34)—dormant because the temporary goal you were pursuing was to answer a question of fact (like, "Is this a good seed?"). Once you've achieved that goal, there is no further need to exercise your faith. But even then, Alma is quick to remind us that "neither must ye lay aside your faith" (verse 36). This is because the ultimate goal or purpose of faith—becoming like Christ—is incomplete. Arguably, that ultimate purpose can never be complete until the work of redemption is done. Thus, knowledge might complement faith. But it won't replace faith in the way that knowledge replaces mere belief.

Another way to see this is to pay attention to the consummation of faith. A careless reading of the sermon might lead one to believe that the consummate form of faith is "perfect knowledge." So let's briefly review the allegory. Alma's target audience consists of people (like the Zoramites) who neither know that the word is a good seed nor believe that it is a good seed. Alma asks those people to trust the Son of God (i.e., to plant the word of the coming of Christ in their hearts). This is akin to asking a gardener to plant a mystery seed in her fruit garden. Imagine that the gardener faces a dilemma: for all she knows, the seed might produce a noxious weed. But imagine also that her garden is already a bit of a disaster. It is not particularly fruitful, and the fruits it does produce are often bitter. If that's her situation, then the gardener's stubbornness of heart (i.e., refusing to plant the seed until she has a perfect knowledge that it is the best plant for her garden) would be an unreasonable and potentially self-undermining attitude. So the virtue of a gardener in such a position would be humility (a receptive openness to good seeds) combined with a vigilance (being alert and watchful, constantly monitoring the growth of the seed to see if it is a good one). If the gardener can determine once and for all that the seed is a good one—if she can achieve a perfect knowledge that the seed is good—this would be a good thing. Not because the knowledge is an end in itself. Knowing that the seed is good won't feed the gardener. Knowledge won't mean that she can stop doing all the things that a good gardener does to plant and nourish and tend her garden. But knowledge would allow her to relax her vigilance, plant more of the seed, and do all the other things a good gardener does. Knowledge would complement her faith; not replace it.

Returning now to Alma's discussion of knowledge, we can see that Alma urges vigilance in just the way we've supposed a good gardener would. The oft-repeated refrain in the sermon—"Is your knowledge perfect?"—is his encouragement to watchfulness in making sure that the seed is good. By exercising faith, Alma's gardener of the heart acquires a direct experience that secures knowledge of very specific propositions. First, I can know that the seed is good in the sense that it grows—I experience directly that it contains the potential to change me. Second, I can know that the seed is good in the sense that it begins to change my heart in good ways: "Your understanding doth *begin* to be enlightened, and your mind doth *begin* to expand" (verse 34; emphasis supplied). But this is not a "perfect" or "complete" knowledge because I don't yet have an absolute certainty that the life of faith is good. Interestingly enough, Alma never claims in the sermon that the gardener who is experimenting on the word manages to achieve a perfect knowledge of the word: "And now behold, after ye have tasted this light is your knowledge perfect? Behold I say unto you, Nay" (verses 35–36).

What the gardener can hope for, however, is enjoyment of the fruits of faith:

Because of your diligence and your faith and
your patience with the word in nourishing it,

that it may take root in you, behold, by and by ye shall pluck the fruit thereof, which is most precious, which is sweet above all that is sweet, and which is white above all that is white, yea, and pure above all that is pure; and ye shall feast upon this fruit even until ye are filled, that ye hunger not, neither shall ye thirst (verse 42).

In the scriptures, hunger and thirst signify a state of despair—an inability to satisfy our most defining desires and needs. So the ultimate vindication and confirmation of faith is not achieved through knowledge[8] but through joy in this world and freedom from despair.

section d: joy as proof

In the original, 1830 edition of the Book of Mormon, Alma's encounter with Korihor and his mission to the Zoramites are both part of a single chapter.[9] There's reason to believe that the chapter breaks in the 1830 edition reflected the chapter organization established by Mormon himself.[10] If that is correct, then, Mormon had a reason for combining in one chapter Alma's very different responses to the atheist Korihor and the God-worshipping Zoramites. The encounter with Korihor frames and informs our understanding of the mission to the Zoramites. The one doctrinal element that Korihor and the Zoramites have in common is this: they both insist "that there shall be no Christ" (compare Alma 30:12 and Alma 31:16). Thus the consistent challenge Alma faces throughout this chapter in the original edition of the Book of Mormon is explaining why someone should accept the doctrine of the coming of Christ. How much certainty should we demand before devoting ourselves to the Christ? Should we wait until we have a surety of knowledge? Should we at least have sufficient evidence to warrant belief—a bare cognitive assent to it? And if we do commit ourselves to the doctrine of the coming of Christ, what kind of reassurance can we hope for that we've done the right thing?

Korihor demands an intellectually satisfying response to such questions. "Then will I be convinced of the truth of thy words" (Alma 30:43), Korihor insists, only if Alma can produce evidence that demonstrates that there is a powerful God. Absent such a proof, he says, "I will deny" that God exists (verse 45). As we saw in chapter 3, Alma does respond to Korihor's demands for cognitively evaluable evidence. He offers his own testimony, the testimony of the prophets, and the testimony of "all things." And, in the end, Korihor even gets his sign.

But in dealing with Korihor, Alma also signals that there is another way to approach the cognitivist demand for evidence and proof. When first brought before Alma, Korihor

> did revile against the priests and teachers,
> accusing them of leading away the people after
> the silly traditions of their fathers, for the sake
> of glutting on the labors of the people (verse 31).

Alma naturally denies this attack on his character by pointing out that he has never made any money at all from his ministry. He concludes his denial with an intriguing question. "Believest thou," Alma asks Korihor, "that we deceive this people, and that causes such joy in their hearts?"[11] (verses 34–35) Alma suggests, in other words, that a false faith, a faith grounded in a deception, could not cause the kind of joy that the members of the church of God experience. Alma doesn't pursue this line of thought with Korihor, but he picks it up again in the Sermon on the Seed.

In fact, Alma is not the first person to respond to Korihor in this way. Before Korihor is brought before Alma, the high priest Giddonah in the land of Gideon

66

also responds to Korihor's attack on the doctrine of the coming of Christ with the question, "Why do ye teach this people that there shall be no Christ, to interrupt their rejoicings?" (verse 22) It is as if Alma and Giddonah think that a feeling of joy alone is sufficient evidence to demonstrate that the doctrine of Christ's coming is true. Of course a hard-core cognitivist like Korihor is not going to be convinced by this kind of evidence. How is joy or any other emotion relevant to the question whether there is adequate evidence to convince the mind of the truth of some claim? The appeal to joy undoubtedly strikes Korihor as more evidence of a "frenzied mind" (verse 16). But with this appeal to the "joy in the hearts" of the faithful, Alma gives us an early indication of the way that he wants to sidestep the cognitivist challenge to a life of faith.

Korihor's aggressive cognitivism is shared by the Zoramite religion, the practices of which consist largely of the Zoramites reciting what they believe and know. One might expect Alma to respond to them in the same way he responded to Korihor—with, for instance, an argument or a sign in support of the doctrine of the coming of Christ. After all, the confrontation with Korihor was, at least temporarily, successful in reinforcing belief in Christ. After news of Korihor's fate was "published throughout all the land" (verse 57), we're told that the people "were all convinced of the wickedness of Korihor; therefore they were all converted again unto the Lord" (verse 58). But this conversion was evidently ephemeral. Shortly "after the end of Korihor,"[12] the Zoramite apostasy breaks out.

It is not surprising then that Alma, in his mission to the Zoramites, adopted a new approach. We've now seen that the "proof" that Alma offers to the Zoramites who doubt the doctrine of the coming of Christ is not knowledge. It is freedom from despair—a release from desires that can never be filled and a satisfaction of the hunger and thirst for righteousness (Alma 32:42). In confronting Korihor, Alma's initial impulse was to point to the joy experienced by the faithful. To the Zoramites, Alma's Sermon offers a road map that concludes with a promise that joy is in their reach:

> And now, my brethren, I desire that ye shall plant this word in your hearts, and as it beginneth to swell even so nourish it by your faith. And behold, it will become a tree, springing up in you unto everlasting life. And then may God grant unto you that your burdens may be light, through the joy of his Son. And even all this can ye do if ye will. Amen. (Alma 33:23)

Joy is the experience of a practical stance that is successfully oriented to the world through Christ. So the confirmation of faith is found in joy. In joy, I have a successful practical hold on existence—free of despair—rather than a cognitive surety about a proposition.

PART II

Alma on Justice and Mercy

In Part I, we reviewed at some length Alma's response to skeptical challenges to the faith. Despite all their differences, Korihor and the Zoramites agreed on one thing: both held that belief in Christ is rationally unwarranted. We have seen that Alma by and large sidestepped the question of the rational justification for belief in Christ. Faith in Christ, Alma taught in the Sermon on the Seed, precedes and is more important than belief or knowledge about Christ.

There is another aspect of Korihor's and the Zoramites' attack on the doctrine of the coming of Christ that we have not yet considered. Both claimed that one great advantage of their skepticism is liberation from "the foolish traditions of your fathers"— traditions that "teach this people to bind themselves down under the foolish ordinances and performances which are laid down by ancient priests, to usurp power and authority over them"[1] (Alma 30:23).

Both lines of attack on religious life are alive and well in the modern world. Belief in God is not only rationally unwarranted, critics maintain, but pernicious because it subjects us to burdensome and harmful traditions. In this view, obedience to religious ordinances and practices is moral immaturity, a failure to take responsibility for oneself, "childishness" (Alma 31:16; see also Alma 30:31 on "the silly traditions of their fathers"). Curiously, some defenders of religious life offer a response that is in fact a mere photographic negative of this criticism. They treat blind obedience— childlike submission—as the ultimate virtue. They argue that God wants obedience for its own sake, and thus they valorize the very kind of blind obedience that skeptics criticize. In the end, then, the only difference between such defenders and their critics consists in whether they reject or valorize the failure to take responsibility for understanding the law.

Neither Alma nor Amulek advocates blind obedience. The law has a purpose, and we are supposed to recognize and understand that purpose. "Behold," Amulek teaches, "this is the whole meaning of the law, every whit pointing to that great and last sacrifice; and that great and last sacrifice will be the Son of God, yea, infinite and eternal" (Alma 34:14). A *whit* is "the smallest part or particle imaginable."[2] Every part and aspect of the law, Amulek maintains, exists to point us toward the sacrifice of the Son of God. The problem with blind obedience is that it is blind also to the meaning of the law. Without insight into that meaning, obedience is literally pointless.

The important question, then, is this: What form does insight into the "whole meaning of the law" take? Is it enough to recognize the meaning with our minds? Is it some form of belief—perhaps the belief that the sacrifice of the Son is infinite and eternal? Alma and Amulek give a different answer. As we will see, they teach that understanding the meaning of the law amounts to learning to be merciful, to exercise mercy in our day-to-day lives. A practical stance centered on mercy is the culmination of Christian life.

5

Faith unto Repentance

Alma delivers the Sermon on the Seed in response to a question. The poorest class of the Zoramites find themselves unable to worship God in the Zoramite fashion because they have been barred from their synagogues. They send a representative to Alma to ask, "What shall we do?" (Alma 32:5). They undoubtedly expect some concrete guidance on how they can continue to worship.

As we saw in chapter 4, Alma's initial answer to their straightforward question is indirect. When he does finally answer the question, his advice is to "experiment upon my words" and "give place that a seed may be planted in your heart" (verses 27–28). Perhaps hoping for something a little less metaphorical, the Zoramites send Alma three follow-up questions. The second question is, "How should they plant the seed?" The third question is, "In what manner should they begin to exercise their faith?" But let's start with Alma and Amulek's answer to the first question, "Should they believe in one God?" (Alma 33:1).

The point of the question might seem obvious. Up until this point in the Sermon on the Seed, Alma has not told the Zoramites which word they should plant in their hearts. He has not so much as mentioned the words *Christ* or *the Son of God*. So on one level, the Zoramites are simply checking to be sure that Alma is inviting them to make an experiment on belief in God. But of course they already believe in God—they are there because they want to worship God in their familiar manner. This suggests that there is something deeper going on with the question.

section a: Alma and the "one God" controversy
The peculiarly worded question—"Should we believe in one God?"—has a bite that is easily missed. To appreciate what is going on here, we need to pay attention to Alma's and Amulek's history with the phrase *one God*. This phrase had been at the very center of a high-stakes theological conflict that had embroiled Alma and Amulek during their mission to the land of Ammonihah (see Alma chapters 10–14).

The "one God" controversy grew out of Zeezrom's attempt (before his conversion) to trap Alma and Amulek in a theological contradiction. Zeezrom laid his snare with an apparently innocuous question:

> Zeezrom said: "Thou sayest there is a true and living God?" And Amulek said: "Yea, there is a true and living God." Now Zeezrom said: "Is there more than one God?" And he answered, "No." (Alma 11:26–29)

As soon as Amulek confessed a monotheistic belief in one God, Zeezrom sprang his trap. He asked Amulek about the doctrine of the coming of Christ:

> And Zeezrom said again: "Who is he that shall come? Is it the Son of God?" And [Amulek] said unto him, "Yea." ... Now Zeezrom said unto the people: "See that ye remember these things; for he said there is but one God; yet he saith that the Son of God shall come." (verses 32–33, 35)

This supposed contradiction provided the basis for charging Amulek with lying (which was a crime under Nephite law; see Alma 1:17).

> The more part of [the people of Ammonihah] were desirous that they might destroy Alma and Amulek; ... and they also said that Amulek

had lied unto them;...And the people went forth and witnessed against them—testifying that [Amulek] had...testified that there was but one God, and that he should send his Son among the people. (Alma 14:2, 5)

It is obvious to the people of Ammonihah that you cannot consistently believe both that there is one God only and that God has a Son. In laying the trap, Zeezrom perhaps reasoned that Amulek's contradiction would lead to an easy conviction for lying. After all, if someone makes two contradictory claims, at least one of them must be false. Thus, if a speaker knowingly asserts a contradiction, that provides prima facie evidence that the speaker is lying. Of course, Amulek was not lying. Ever since the days of Nephi himself, the Nephite faithful had affirmed that the Father, Son, and Holy Ghost are "one God" (see 2 Ne. 31:21; Alma 11:44). Perhaps this doctrine was so familiar that they scarcely noticed its oxymoronic character. But it is not surprising that the people of Ammonihah saw in it a contradiction, and it is interesting to note that neither Alma nor Amulek make any effort to dispel the paradox.[1]

In any event, when the Zoramites ask whether they should believe in the "one God," that precise phrase seems to be deliberately chosen to invoke the earlier controversy.[2] By referring to Alma's doctrine in this way, the Zoramites highlight the difficulties they experience in believing in one God who is three persons.

Once we recognize that the "one God" controversy lies behind the Zoramites' question, we can see new depths in Alma's response. When the Zoramites ask whether they should believe in "one God," Alma's immediate response is to invoke the scriptural authority of Zenos and Zenock, who both write about the Son of God.[3] He completes the sermon by drawing an analogy between Moses's brazen serpent and the doctrine of the coming of Christ. In the Book of Mormon tradition, a number of Israelites refused to look to Moses's brazen serpent.[4] Why? Well, perhaps it seemed incoherent to the Israelites that the God of the third commandment would now give them a "graven image," let alone tell them to look to it for healing.[5] "The reason [the Israelites] would not look," Alma explains, "is because they did not believe that it would heal them" (Alma 33:20). But—and this is Alma's point—whether the idea of the serpent made intellectual sense[6] to them should have been inconsequential in the face of the fact of their healing. Similarly, the doctrine of the coming of Christ, the "one God" doctrine, may not make rational sense to the Zoramites. But worries about that incoherence will fade in importance if faith in Christ heals and redeems them. Alma's proposed experiment is as simple as looking up at the brazen serpent: trust the doctrine of the coming of Christ and see what effects that has on your way of life. Alma's "argument" in favor of the "one God" doctrine is: "Look and live"! (verse 19).

section b: Amulek and the "expediency" argument
Like Alma, Amulek does not address, let alone resolve, the theological question of how God's three persons can be one God. Instead, he cuts right to the core issue:

> We have beheld that the great question which
> is in your minds is whether the word be in the
> Son of God, or whether there shall be no Christ.
> (Alma 34:5)

Notice that this is a question in their *minds*—the Zoramites are still approaching this as a matter of belief rather than faith. Amulek makes explicit what was tacitly hinted at in the Zoramites' question. "There shall be no Christ"—that is what both Korihor (Alma 30:22) and the Zoramite priests taught (Alma 31:16). So Amulek, like Alma, recognizes that they are really asking, Should they continue to believe in the impersonal God of the Zoramite religion? Or should they devote themselves to the Son of God, and thereby to a God who is one and many at the same time—a conception of God that seems incoherent to them given their preexisting cognitive commitments?

Because Amulek sees that the Zoramites still have intellectual doubts, he offers an argument in support of the doctrine of the coming of Christ. As we will see, this is not because Amulek wants the Zoramites merely to believe that the Son of God will come. He, like Alma, wants them to adopt a practical stance of faith in Christ. But the argument might perform an important service if it can remove a mental obstacle to acting in faith.

The Zoramites reject the doctrine of the coming of Christ on intellectual grounds. They do not believe that God can change, and thus they do not believe that God can take on human form. Amulek addresses those doubts directly:

> Christ shall come among the children of men, to take upon him the transgressions of his people, and that he shall atone for the sins of the world. . . . For it is expedient that an atonement should be made. (Alma 34:8–9)

The word *expedient* is crucial to Amulek's argument. As Amulek uses the word, and as it is used more broadly in the Book of Mormon, something is *expedient* when it helps us achieve some purpose but is not in and of itself sufficient to achieve that purpose. For example, you could say that gasoline is expedient to driving a car. Without the gasoline, there is no hope of driving anywhere. But filling the tank with gasoline is not alone sufficient to make the car run—you also need a live battery and working spark plugs, and so on.

It is in this sense that the atonement is expedient to the salvation of humankind. It alone cannot save us—it also takes repentance on our part. But without the atonement, there is no hope of our being redeemed from our fallen state. Since "a great and last sacrifice" (Alma 34:13) is the enabling condition of our salvation, Amulek concludes that we can trust that God will come in the flesh because that is the only way the necessary atonement can be made. Here is his argument:

> According to the great plan of the Eternal God there must be an atonement made, or else all mankind must unavoidably perish; yea, all are hardened; yea, all are fallen and are lost, and must perish except it be through the atonement which it is expedient should be made. (Alma 34:9)

Let's unpack this argument a little bit. Amulek's reasoning hinges on two key suppositions. First, that beings are "hardened," and "fallen and lost." A heart is "hardened" when one is no longer responsive to the needs of others or to God's invitation to do good. When human beings are hardened, they are willful and selfish and thus incapable of adopting the practical stance of faith. "Fallen and lost" means alienated from God. People who are fallen and lost pursue their carnal desires and live without a sense for the sacred in the world. We can call this hardened, lost condition "fallenness" for short.

Amulek's second key supposition is that people in a state of fallenness cannot through their own efforts reconcile themselves to God. From this it follows that if reconciliation is to come, it will have to come from an extra-human source: "It is expedient that there should be a great and last sacrifice," and this sacrifice "shall not be a human sacrifice; but it must be an infinite and eternal sacrifice" (verse 10).

There are two different ways to understand the infinite and the eternal. The first interpretation—I'll

call this the pop-theological interpretation—understands the "infinite" as something that is unmeasurably
large in expanse, the "eternal" as something unmeasurably long in duration. This way of understanding the
infinite sacrifice lends itself to an economic interpretation of Amulek's claim. The reason that God has to
sacrifice himself is that he alone has enough value to
pay off all the moral debts of the entire human race.
No finite human's sacrifice is enough to make good on
what we owe to God as a result of our transgression.

But the terms *infinite* and *eternal* and *endless* are not
used in the book of Alma in the way that the pop-theological interpretation understands them. Perhaps the
best demonstration of this is Alma's experience when
confronted in his youth by the angel. "For the space
of three days and three nights," Alma notes, "I was
racked with eternal torment" (Alma 36:10, 12). An eternal torment that lasted for three days? Clearly, either
Alma is guilty of over-the-top exaggeration, or *eternal*
here is not synonymous with "going on forever." The
latter is the case. Another example is Moroni's claim
that the resurrection "bringeth to pass a redemption
from an endless sleep, from which sleep all men shall
be awakened by the power of God" (Morm. 9:13). This
is a self-contradictory claim to make if *endless* means
"going on forever"; there is no waking up from a sleep
that goes on forever. What is going on in such passages?

When something is described as *eternal* in the
book of Alma, it means that the eternal thing is incapable of being diminished by time. In other words, not
that it actually does exist forever, but it could exist forever without changing in any essential respect.[7] Thus
Alma's eternal torment was a sort of torment that Alma
could never get used to, no matter how long it lasted.
Conversely, an eternal happiness would be a happiness
that no amount of time would diminish—a happiness

that never gets old, never becomes tedious, never stops being happiness. Similarly, when something is *infinite*, this means that it is incommensurable with any finite amount of something else. There is no quantity of finite goods (money, pleasure, etc.) that could be exchanged for something infinite—not because the infinite is worth an unimaginably large amount of such goods, but because it is the wrong sort of thing to be exchanged for finite things. If someone would seriously entertain the question, "How much money is a human being worth?"—that person fails to recognize the infinite character of humanity. And this is perhaps the ultimate reason why our redemption requires an infinite and eternal sacrifice. We have fallen, neglecting our infinite worth and injuring ourselves and each other for finite pleasures and gains. "For thus saith the Lord: Ye have sold yourselves for naught, and ye shall be redeemed without money" (3 Ne. 20:38; Isa. 52:3). God's infinite sacrifice does not mean a huge sacrifice or an unimaginably painful sacrifice (although, of course, it might be huge and incredibly painful as well); it means a sacrifice that has no "cash" or exchange value in terms of measurable pleasure and pain.

As Amulek points out, the economic model of atonement has one significant flaw: it assumes that one person can pay someone else's moral debt. If I steal from you, someone else can restore the money to you. But, in doing so, they do not fix my relationship to you, and they cannot make it the case that I am not a thief. I have to change myself and make amends to you—no one else can do that for me. Thus, Amulek notes, "there is not any man that can sacrifice his own blood which will atone for the sins of another" (Alma 34:11). He concludes: "It is expedient that there should be a great and last sacrifice" (verse 13). The pop-theological interpretation understands Amulek as invoking a kind of supernatural power on the part of the Christ: no man can atone for another, but somehow a God can. I take Amulek's point to be different: because no one can atone for the sins of another, we need to stop thinking in terms of the payment of debts. We need to focus on how to heal the relationships between us.

In other words, the "great and last sacrifice" (verses 10, 13) is the last sacrifice because it is meant to put an end to the domination of an economic model of justice that had prevailed up until that point. The law was given to train us in a godly form of life. A punishment was affixed to the law to try to restore, to some degree, a state of justice that is lost when people do wrong. But in doing wrong, we do an infinite wrong, harming ourselves, others, and God. When something of truly infinite and eternal worth is injured through our transgression, no finite economy of paying debts and suffering punishments can repair the harm. There is no quantitative way to measure what we owe the ones whom we harm, and no way to repay them fully through finite offerings and acts of obedience. If there is to be a way out of fallenness, then, it has to come by overcoming the entire economic model of justice. In sacrificing himself for us, God suffers an infinite and eternal harm because of us. In recognizing this, we are jolted out of an economic mindset. We see that there is no hope of repaying what God has sacrificed for us.

Amulek does not describe the mechanics of the atonement. He never offers a theory of how it works. But he does explain what happens when it does work:

And thus he shall bring salvation to all those who shall believe on his name; this being the intent of this last sacrifice, to bring about the bowels of mercy, which overpowereth justice, and bringeth about means unto men that they may have faith unto repentance. (verse 15)

The emphasis on the bowels of mercy is significant. The bowels are the seat of our most powerful passions— anger, lust, and (as here) mercy or compassion. This is not merely a metaphorical expression; we literally feel powerful passions deep inside our body. Thus, Alma explains that the path to repentance is opened up by a change I can feel in the innermost core of my body. To truly understand my guilt before the law and God's sacrifice for me, I have to feel them in my gut. The intent of God's sacrifice is to produce in us a powerful yearning to show mercy and receive mercy. To be in a merciful state of *mind* is not enough. There are some things the mind cannot grasp on its own because thought is too detached, too cool, too dispassionate. Transformative mercy is one of them.

The point of the law, in other words, is to prepare us to understand viscerally Christ's sacrifice for us. And when the atonement has worked, we do feel that powerful, deep mercy. We are moved to show the same kind of compassion for others that Christ has shown to us. It is worth reflecting on just how different this view of the law is from the ones we canvassed previously. In blind obedience to the law, obedience for its own sake, we cede responsibility over ourselves to the law. By contrast, an understanding submission to the law makes us merciful to our core. The ends of the law are fulfilled when we own responsibility for ourselves—indeed, we go beyond our legal obligations and take it upon ourselves to heal more than we are responsible for. Thus obedience to the law, and the law itself, has a purely instrumental function—it is a means, and mercy is the end.

To sum it all up, then, Amulek's argument is this: Humans are too lost and hardhearted to reconcile themselves to God. The only hope for reconciliation is for God to take on human form and offer himself as a sacrifice. This has the power to soften our hardened hearts. Remember, at this point the question is not, has Amulek offered a rational proof that will secure the belief that Christ will atone for us? The question is, Has he opened up enough space in the hearts of the Zoramites for them to plant the word?

section c: the remaining questions
As we noted at the outset of this chapter, the Zoramites had three follow-up questions for Alma. We've looked so far at the answer to the question whether they should believe in one God. Alma and Amulek together encouraged them to experiment on the "one God" doctrine—that God is Father, Son, and Holy Spirit, and in the person of the Son of God will come to redeem his people. But what of the other questions—How should they plant the seed?, and In what manner should they begin to exercise their faith (Alma 33:1)?

Alma leaves it to Amulek to answer these questions. His answer is straightforward: they should plant the seed in their heart by trusting in God and by learning to see God's hand in all things. Amulek instructs them to do this by practicing a form of prayer that is constant, humble, and other-regarding. This is in marked contrast to the Zoramite practice of prayer, which was practiced once a week and in a way that elevated the self and reviled others! Amulek's model of prayer involves continuous humility and pleading with God for mercy (Alma 34:17–19), and it involves learning to see all good things—fields and flocks, houses and households, and all aspects of "your welfare" and "the welfare of those around you"—as gifts from God (verses 20–21, 24–27).

In what manner should they begin to exercise faith? Amulek's answer is, "Humble yourselves even to the dust" and "live in thanksgiving daily, for the many mercies and blessings which he doth bestow upon you" (verse 38). This takes the concrete form of putting ourselves to work in the service of others—taking in the needy, clothing the naked, visiting the sick, giving to the poor: "I say unto you, if ye do not any of these things, behold, your prayer is vain, and availeth you nothing, and ye are as hypocrites who do deny the faith" (verse 28).

6

The Phenomenology of Anguish and Mercy

The defining event in the life of Alma the Younger—the event that transformed his understanding of himself and of his relationship to God and to the world—was an event of unexpected, overwhelming mercy. This experience was so significant for Alma, and for his understanding of the doctrine of the coming of Christ, that it is recounted three separate times in the Book of Mormon—once in Mosiah chapter 27, again in Alma 36, and once more for good measure in Alma 38.

Alma picks out two distinct moments of the Lord's saving mercy. First, that "the Lord in his great mercy sent his angel to declare unto me that I must stop the work of destruction among his people" (Alma 38:7). God had, through Alma's father and through the scriptures and prophecies, already warned Alma amply of the consequences of his actions. It was an act of mercy (one that most people do not enjoy) to deliver a final warning through an angel.

The second moment of mercy that Alma experienced during that fateful confrontation with the angel was the transformative mercy of forgiveness. In the Alma chapter 36 version, he describes at great length the "eternal torment" and "pains of hell" that accompanied his conviction of guilt:

> So great had been my iniquities, that the very thought of coming into the presence of my God did rack my soul with inexpressible horror. Oh,

thought I, that I could be banished and become extinct both soul and body, that I might not... be judged of my deeds. (Alma 26:12–15)

In the depths of his despair, Alma grasps at the only remaining source of hope:

> I remembered also to have heard my father prophesy unto the people concerning the coming of one Jesus Christ, a Son of God, to atone for the sins of the world. Now, as my mind caught hold upon this thought, I cried within my heart: O Jesus, thou Son of God, have mercy on me, who am in the gall of bitterness, and am encircled about by the everlasting chains of death. And now, behold, when I thought this, I could remember my pains no more; yea, I was harrowed up by the memory of my sins no more. (verses 17–19)

The immediate forgiveness and release from suffering that Alma experienced is surely one of the most dramatic examples of God's mercy in the Book of Mormon.

Notice the temporal structure, or the dimension of time, in Alma's description. His present moment of suffering is shaped by his memories of the past ("I did remember all my sins and iniquities") and his anticipation of the future ("the everlasting chains of death"). His experience of mercy is described as an experience of a change to that temporal structure—a changed past (he is "harrowed up by the memory of my sins no more") and a changed future (he now anticipates "the coming of one Jesus Christ, a Son of God, to atone for the sins of the world"). The second type of mercy could be thought of as an unexpected but welcome change to the temporal structure of his present existence.

The temporal structure that Alma describes points to a third type of mercy. As we will see in chapter 8, the temporal space of human mortal existence is in itself a gift of God's grace. It is an act of mercy on God's part to grant "a time . . . unto man to repent" (Alma 42:4).

These three types of divine mercy point to a common core that defines merciful acts in general. A merciful act is an act in which person A relieves the suffering of person B—either by enabling B to avoid the suffering him- or herself, or by acting to lift the suffering. In all the cases of mercy that we find in the book of Alma, B fully deserves to suffer as a consequence of B's transgression. And so A acts without regard to questions of desert. Finally, in each case, A is motivated by compassion for B: "the bowels of mercy" that characterize divine acts of mercy are an immediate, deeply felt motivation to relieve the suffering of others.[1] So we can define a merciful act in this way:

> A *merciful act* is an action in which A relieves B's suffering without regard to desert, and A is motivated by compassion for B's suffering.

Alma's many-faceted experience of God's mercy shapes his life and ministry. For one thing, it convinces him of the ephemeral nature of carnal pleasures. It is undoubtedly on the basis of his confrontation with the angel that Alma warns his son Corianton that "if it were not for the plan of redemption, (laying it aside), as soon as [human beings] were dead their souls were miserable, being cut off from the presence of the Lord" (Alma 42:11). After all, during those three days and nights, Alma himself had a prior glimpse of what spiritual death (that is, being "cut off from the presence of the Lord" [verse 9]) is like for the unredeemed soul. As long as we are alive, our days are filled up with all manner of distractions—the strivings, pleasures, and hopes of everyday activities. If we can distract ourselves with such transient concerns, then we don't notice how empty existence is without a relationship to God or without sacred relations to others. Once those distractions and their accompanying pleasures are gone, however, we are confronted with the person we have made ourselves into, and there is no avoiding the indelible memory of the injuries we have inflicted through selfishness and sin.

Alma's vivid memory of his experience of "the pains of a damned soul" (Alma 36:16) drives his unflagging efforts to convince people of the doctrine of the coming of Christ. He is motivated by a desire to spare others from that suffering and to let them experience the joy he felt when he finally did receive God's mercy:

> From that time even until now, I have labored
> without ceasing, that I might bring souls unto
> repentance; that I might bring them to taste of
> the exceeding joy of which I did taste. (verse 24)

But he is also motivated by an enduring sense that the mercy he received is something he did not deserve. Alma is very much aware that he deserved "eternal torment," "the pains of hell," "inexpressible horrors," and the "gall of bitterness" (verses 12–14, 18). As he later instructs Corianton, it is vital that he "should deny the justice of God no more. Do not endeavor to excuse yourself in the least point because of your sins, by denying the justice of God; but do you let the justice of God, and his mercy, and his long-suffering have full sway in your heart; and let it bring you down to the dust in humility" (Alma 42:30). In Alma's experience, mercy can be correctly understood only if it is accompanied by a full recognition of one's just condemnation under the law.

And so Alma's confrontation with the angel gives birth to the most distinctive feature of Alma's ministry: his emphasis on mercy as the ultimate goal and perfection of human existence. Alma's doctrine places the conflict between justice and mercy at the heart of human redemption. We will look in the next chapter at Alma's account of the ultimate harmony that can be achieved between justice and mercy through the mediation of Christ. But first, let's briefly review earlier Book of Mormon accounts of the relationship between justice and mercy. This will highlight the distinctive character of Alma's doctrine.

The Book of Mormon opens with Lehi's call as a prophet. In a vision, Lehi is given a book to read containing God's judgment and the impending destruction of Jerusalem (1 Ne. 1:13). Lehi's immediate reaction, however, is to declare that God's "power, and goodness, and mercy are over all the inhabitants of the earth; and, because thou art merciful, thou wilt not suffer those who come unto thee that they shall perish!" (1 Ne. 1:14). For Lehi, both the just enforcement of the law and mercy are recognized as being among God's principal attributes. He treats justice and mercy as complementary and mutually compatible attributes (see, e.g., 2 Ne. 2:5, 8).

Similarly, Jacob taught that mercy could claim those who had not received the law (2 Ne. 9:25–26). For the rest, justice must be executed (2 Ne 9:17). Nevertheless, God in his mercy will save "as many as will not harden their hearts" (Jacob 6:4–5). One finds in Jacob no discussion of any conflict between the necessary execution of God's justice and his mercy in "deliver[ing] his saints from that awful monster the devil, and death, and hell" (2 Ne. 9:17–19). Justice and mercy appear to work together seamlessly.

King Benjamin likewise describes eloquently both God's justice and his mercy in relation to his children. As Benjamin explains it, mercy operates within the bounds of justice (see Mosiah 3:24–26). Here again, there is no acknowledgment of a potential for conflict between the demands of justice and the claim of mercy. These two attributes of God operate in a complementary way. Justice condemns the unrepentant to punishment (Mosiah 2:38). "Mercy," Benjamin notes, "hath no claim on that man" (verse 39). Meanwhile, mercy and justice together reward those who "abound in good works" (Mosiah 5:15).

Starting with Abinadi, however, a subtle change appears in the way that mercy and justice are treated. Rather than casting them as complementary traits of God's nature, Abinadi describes the Son of God as "standing betwixt [the children of men] and justice" (Mosiah 15:9) because he "ha[s] the bowels of mercy; being filled with compassion towards the children of men" (verse 9). The "bowels of mercy"—a visceral, powerfully felt impulse to relieve our suffering—are manifest when the Son "take[s] upon himself [our] iniquity and [our] transgressions" (verse 9). As Abinadi understands it, then, Christ sets himself as a barrier between us and the justice of God. God has "giv[en] the Son power to make intercession for the children of men" (verse 8).

And yet, Abinadi concludes, "having redeemed them," the Son "satisfied the demands of justice" (verse 9). There is just a hint of paradox in this passage. If the Son has satisfied the demands of justice for us, why would he have to set himself between us and justice? Or perhaps it is in the merciful act of setting himself between us and justice that the Son satisfies the demands of justice? Abinadi leaves such questions unanswered.

In the doctrine of Alma and his companions, this paradox is emphasized as they attempt to articulate their firsthand experience of tension between the demands of justice and the mercy of Christ. For example, Ammon recalls for his brothers the confrontation with the angel that had transformed both them and Alma. Ammon asks with some amazement:

Who could have supposed that our God would have been so merciful as to have snatched us from our awful, sinful, and polluted state?

Behold, we went forth even in wrath, with mighty threatenings to destroy his church. Oh then, why did he not consign us to an awful destruction, yea, why did he not let the sword of his justice fall upon us, and doom us to eternal despair? Oh, my soul, almost as it were, fleeth at the thought. *Behold, he did not exercise his justice upon us*, but in his great mercy hath brought us over that everlasting gulf of death and misery, even to the salvation of our souls (Alma 26:17–20; emphasis supplied).

In Ammon's telling, Christ's mercy prevents the exercise of justice or holds the judgments under the law in abeyance. Ammon acknowledges immediately the paradox involved in this claim: "And now behold, my brethren, what natural man is there that knoweth these things? I say unto you, there is none that knoweth these things, save it be the penitent" (Alma 26:21).

As we saw in the previous chapter, Amulek describes the relationship between justice and mercy in even more conflictual terms. Mercy does not merely prevent the exercise of justice, it "overpowereth justice" (Alma 34:15). To "overpower" something is to defeat it, to vanquish it, to subdue it with overwhelming force. Nevertheless, Amulek immediately goes on to explain, that "mercy can satisfy the demands of justice" (verse 16).

It is left to Alma to develop a detailed account of how this reconciliation is to occur. Let's turn now to Alma's doctrine of justice and mercy.

7

Justice and Mercy

As we saw in the previous chapter, Alma's conversion to faith in Christ was accompanied by his experience of the disparity between the judgment he deserved and the mercy he received. Alma had a powerful and personal awareness of a tension between justice and mercy. This tension generated the motivational force that launched Alma into the ministry. Alma, more than any other prophet, sees the tension between justice and mercy not as a contradiction to be resolved but as a powerful impetus to Christian life. Alma's explanation of the reconciliation between justice and mercy is designed to harness the tension, not to dissolve or release it.

Before looking at Alma's account of the reconciliation of justice and mercy, however, let's try first to spell out the reason for the tension that exists between them.

section a: the theological problem of justice and mercy
The theological tradition has long seen a problem in the idea that God is both supremely merciful and perfectly just.[1] The problem is this: a perfectly just being would always give people exactly the punishment they deserve. But a merciful being would relieve people of suffering. So if God is merciful, he cannot be just. And if he is just, he cannot be merciful.

Let's try to formulate the problem a little more precisely. We can define a *state of justice* in this way:

A state of justice is a situation in which each individual has what he or she deserves.

A *just act*, at a minimum, is an action that helps bring about a state of justice. But to be truly just, the act cannot have any ulterior motives (like a desire to be praised). A just act must be motivated by the desire to produce a state of justice. Given our definition of a state of justice, we can define a just act in this way:

> A just act is an action in which some agent A gives to another agent B what B deserves, and in which A is motivated by a desire to produce a state of justice.[2]

Thus, where A must choose between two or more options that differ in the degree to which they give B what B deserves, then A acts justly if and only if A chooses the option that most closely approximates what B deserves.

So, suppose B steals the wallet of some third party, C. Judge A has to choose from among a range of options, including giving the wallet back to C and punishing B, or letting B keep the stolen wallet. A will act justly if she gives C what he deserves—his wallet—and if she gives to B what he deserves—an appropriate punishment for his crime. And, of course, she must be motivated by a desire to bring about a state of justice, rather than being motivated by (for example) a desire to impress onlookers so that she can win an upcoming election.

How about mercy? In chapter 7, we defined an act of mercy in this way:

> A merciful act is an action in which A relieves B's suffering without regard to desert, and A is motivated by compassion for B's suffering.

As this definition emphasizes, it is important that this act be motivated in the right way—namely, by a compassion for the sufferer. For instance, if I act to alleviate the suffering of another because I want you to praise me for my kindness, I'm not truly merciful.

This definition suggests that where A must choose between two or more options that differ in the degree to which they relieve *B*'s suffering, then *A* acts mercifully if and only if ① *A* chooses an option that relieves *B*'s suffering more than at least one other option, and ② *A* is not otherwise obligated to choose that option.[3]

So, for instance, if *C* beats *B* and leaves him by the side of the road where *A* finds him, *A* has at least two options that differ in the degree to which they relieve *B*'s suffering. *A* could pass *B* by and leave him there. Or, *A* could help *B*. *A* acts mercifully if she chooses (for instance) to bind up *B*'s wounds, and get him medical care. This relieves his suffering more than leaving him by the side of the road. But this doesn't count as a merciful act if she is otherwise obligated to help him—say, if she is an EMT and is getting paid to respond to *B*'s emergency.

With these definitions in mind, we can see why there is a high potential for conflict between what justice would require us to do and what mercy would encourage us to do. In fact, the conflict is real in the case of Alma. Alma himself acknowledges that he deserves to be punished for his transgressions (see Alma 36:13–14). We can suppose the following are among God's options: 1 he can either give Alma exactly the punishment that he deserves, or 2 he can give Alma some lesser punishment. Justice requires that God give him the punishment he deserves. Mercy invites God to relieve his suffering. Since Alma deserves punishment for his sins, if God acts justly he cannot show mercy to Alma. And if he acts mercifully, he cannot act justly.

In Alma's case, God shows mercy. In the midst of his suffering—suffering that Alma himself regards as just— he turns to God and immediately receives mercy:

> I cried within my heart: O Jesus, thou Son of God, have mercy on me, who am in the gall of bitterness, and am encircled about by the everlasting chains of death. And now, behold, when I thought this, I could remember my pains no more; yea, I

was harrowed up by the memory of my sins no more. And oh, what joy, and what marvelous light I did behold; yea, my soul was filled with joy as exceeding as was my pain (Alma 36:18–20)!

And then, as if simple forgiveness were not mercy enough, Alma is also immediately rewarded with a celestial vision and by healing in both spirit and body (see verses 22–23). Far more just and righteous people than Alma have longed for such blessings in vain. Alma's case, on the face of it, thus presents a direct contradiction between God's justice and his mercy. God chose mercy—but was it at the expense of justice?

section b: strategies for reconciliation
There are two initially appealing ways to try to reconcile justice and mercy that, upon further reflection, don't really work.

The first approach argues that at least some acts of mercy are compatible with the demands of justice—namely, acts of mercy in just those cases where punishment according to the law is too harsh. This approach to reconciliation supposes that there are some acts of justice—just punishments according to the law—that do not produce a state of justice because the law as applied in certain circumstances does not track desert. On this view, as long as God exercises mercy only to soften an unduly harsh sentence (i.e., in cases where the law does not track desert), mercy will be fully compatible with justice. Indeed, mercy in such cases would enhance justice by encouraging the judge to reduce the punishment to an appropriate level. But this fails as an account of the reconciliation of justice and mercy. For if the law requires an inappropriate punishment, then the law is not in fact just. If the punishment is not just, then justice itself requires God to reduce the punishment. Mercy has no part to play here.

Another strategy proposes that we should show mercy only when the wrongdoer has repented and thus done something to deserve mercy. In Alma's case, for instance, you might think that he has "earned" mercy by starting to repent during his three days of paralyzed anguish. But this does not solve the contradiction, for there are two possibilities: either the repentant sinner now deserves to have her punishment relieved, or she does not. If she, through her repentance, now deserves to have her punishment relieved then it would be unjust to refuse to relieve it. In that case, God's forgiveness of the sinner is not an act of mercy but an act of justice. On the other hand, if the repentant sinner still deserves punishment (say, her repentance has not done enough to warrant complete forgiveness),[4] then it would be unjust not to punish her. In that case, mercy is once again shown to be contrary to justice. It thus does not seem possible that God could be both supremely merciful and perfectly just.

Cases like Alma's thus present us with a genuine tension between God's perfect justice and his mercy. Indeed, as we saw in chapter 7, Alma and his companions repeatedly described their experience as involving something like a contradiction. This was most strikingly evident in Amulek's claim that mercy overpowers justice (Alma 34:15)—as if God's mercy had altogether blocked or defeated an attempt to apply a just punishment.

section c: Alma on the concord between justice and mercy
The most striking feature of Alma's approach to the problem of justice and mercy is that Alma argues for a harmony between justice and mercy that does not depend on eliminating the tension between them. In fact, the relationship between justice and mercy is arguably at its best when the tension is most pronounced. Just as the tension between the string and the bow brings about the

means to shoot an arrow, the tension between justice and mercy "bringeth about means unto men that they may have faith unto repentance" (Alma 34:15).

Thus, Alma advises that you should not even try "to excuse yourself in the least point because of your sins, by denying the justice of God" (Alma 42:30). Mercy overpowers justice, but you still need to feel your guilt: you need simultaneously to "let the justice of God, and his mercy . . . have full sway in your heart, and let it bring you down to the dust in humility" (verse 30). *Sway* in this context means "prevailing, overpowering, or controlling influence."[5] This is thus deeply paradoxical advice. Despite their conflicting ways of treating the sinner, justice and mercy are both somehow to prevail and have overpowering influence. It is precisely the paradoxical tension in undeserved forgiveness that humbles us. We are reoriented practically and emotionally by the simultaneous experience of fully deserving a just punishment and receiving a wholly undeserved gift of mercy. Having discovered the transformative power of loving mercy, we become inclined to extend the same loving mercy to others. This change to our practical stance is what makes it possible for us to repent. Because this change depends on the greatest possible tension between what justice demands and what mercy offers, it would frustrate the plan of redemption if there were to be a complete reconciliation between justice and mercy.

Of course, if mercy is exercised in a way that "destroy[s] the work of justice," then the productive tension is also destroyed. So redemption, the work of mercy,

> could not be brought about, only on conditions
> of repentance of men in this probationary state,
> yea, . . . for except it were for these conditions,
> mercy could not take effect except it should
> destroy the work of justice (Alma 42:13).

So there's still some explaining to be done: How does repentance allow for genuine acts of mercy that do not destroy the work of justice?

Alma's answer involves recognizing a distinction between the function of justice and the aim or purpose of having a system of justice. The function of justice is what it does. The aim of justice is what it is trying to achieve by doing what it does. This might at first seem like a very fine distinction, but it is an important one nonetheless. For example, there is a difference between the function of a knife (what all knives do—cut things) and the aim or purpose of having a knife. There are a variety of purposes I might have for owning a knife. I might buy a knife for slicing vegetables, or for defending myself, or for healing through surgery. Ultimately, the purpose of the knife is more important than the function of the knife—if other things allow us to achieve the purpose as well or better without performing the function, we are happy to dispense with the function. For instance, if a surgeon encounters a case where physical therapy will heal better than surgery, she ought happily to set the surgical knife aside. And it would be silly, in those circumstances, to insist that doctors continue to use surgical knives to treat patients just because knives perform an important function.

How does this distinction between a function and a purpose apply to justice? The function of justice is to create a state of justice. It performs this function by *executing the law*. Alma calls the function of justice "the works of justice"—in the sense that this is the work performed by having and enforcing laws. This is what Alma is referring to when he observes that

> justice claimeth the creature and executeth
> the law, and the law inflicteth the punishment;
> if not so, *the works of justice* would be destroyed
> (Alma 42:22; emphasis supplied).

The function of justice, what justice does—that is, executing the laws—has been our focus so far. We've concentrated on justice as the action of rendering to each person what she deserves under the law. But—and this is a crucial but easily overlooked part of Alma's analysis—creating a state of justice is not God's ultimate aim in giving a law and affixing a punishment to it (verse 22). As Alma explains, justice is in the service of bringing about God's "great and eternal purposes" (verse 26).

So what are the great and eternal purposes for executing the law and enforcing justice? We've already noted the answer. The purpose of justice is to bring us to a state of repentance—that is, to call us to try to transform ourselves out of our natural, sinful, and fallen nature.

> Now, how could a man repent except he should
> sin? How could he sin if there was no law? How
> could there be a law save there was a punish-
> ment? Now, there was a punishment affixed,
> and a just law given, which brought remorse
> of conscience unto man (verses 17–18).

The function of justice, then, is to execute the laws, thereby rendering to each what he or she deserves. The result of God's execution of justice on the day of judgment would be a good thing—a world that approximates as closely as possible a just order, where each gets what he or she deserves, and is deprived of the things they do not deserve. It could not be a fully just order, however, because it could not undo the harm that people inflicted on each other and the injustice that we had to endure while waiting for justice. God can forgive us for the wrongs we have done to him, but he can't forgive us on behalf of each other. Only you can forgive me for hurting you. This consideration points us to a better way: a world where we forgive each other for the wrongs that each inflicts on the others, and we set about trying to relieve the suffering of each other without waiting for a final calculation of what each deserves. What is better than a state of justice? A state of mercy—a state in which each gets more than he or she deserves because each is merciful to the other.

Alma thus explains that justice and mercy can achieve a kind of concord because God's great and eternal purpose for executing the laws is to produce this better way—to "bring remorse of conscience unto man," to "bring us down to the dust in humility" so that we will have "faith unto repentance" (Alma 34:15–17). Remember—faith for Alma is a practical stance, not a cognitive state. Faith unto repentance involves having a humble trust in God, a purposive orientation toward a change in our form of life, a readiness to act as God wants us to act, and feelings of humility and remorse. Faith unto repentance, in a word, is a practical stance devoted to the godly transformation of our natural state.

How in particular, does God want us to transform ourselves?

Now surely, whosoever repenteth shall find
mercy; and he that findeth mercy and endureth
to the end the same shall be saved. (Alma 32:13)

I think that many people read *find* in this passage as "be the recipient of." And that's not wrong—God stands ready to show mercy to those who repent. But this interpretation tells only half the story. *Find* also (and indeed more naturally) means "gain possession of" or "attain" or "arrive" at a particular condition. For example, in describing to his son Shiblon his transformative encounter with the angel, Alma says:

Never, until I did cry out unto the Lord Jesus
Christ for mercy, did I receive a remission of

my sins. But behold, I did cry unto him and I did find peace to my soul (Alma 38:8).

He received mercy in the form of a remission of sins. As a result of that gift, he also found peace—that is, he arrived at a condition of peacefulness. Finding something is not a passive event. It involves effort and change on our part. Finding is attaining a condition as the result of seeking (3 Ne. 14:8). But if finding is not passive, neither is it fully active. Finding is not manufacturing—it's not wholly within the power of the seeker. Finding happens when one (actively) puts oneself into a position to be transformed by what is sought, but whether the transformation occurs depends on that which is sought giving itself to the seeker.

The ultimate purpose of justice, the work that justice aims to produce, is to help us find mercy—not just to receive acts of kindness or pity but to be transformed so that we become merciful. God's ultimate judgment, Alma teaches, consists in a restoration of "[what is] just for that which is just; [what is] merciful for that which is merciful. Therefore," Alma urges us, "see that you are merciful" (Alma 41:13–14). We find mercy when we become beings who no longer seek after our own interests and right but seek instead to compassionately relieve others of their unhappiness without thought for their desert.

When Nephi sought an interpretation of Lehi's vision of the tree, the angel posed him a question: "Knowest thou the condescension of God?" (1 Ne. 11:16). "To condescend" is to willingly surrender your rights and privileges—as Christ does when he forbears punishing us. To know the condescension of God is for us to condescend in a similar way—to willingly forbear from demanding justice of those who have hurt us. For Alma, this is the central lesson of Christianity: the purpose of the law and the aim of repentance is to fill our bowels with mercy to others. Or as Jesus himself put it: "Blessed are the merciful, for they shall obtain mercy" (3 Ne. 12:7).

Thus, when Alma says, "Mercy claimeth all which is her own" (Alma 42:24), that should be heard as saying "Mercy claims all those who are merciful."

God's mercy for the merciful is in tension with, indeed is contrary to, the function of justice. It overpowers and thus prevents the just execution of punishment. But when God's mercy for us helps us become merciful, it achieves the purpose for having a system of justice, and it does so better than the execution of justice alone could. Thus, if we have become merciful, justice has no grounds for complaint when God forgoes executing justice on us. After all, the ultimate purpose of justice has already been realized. When mercy claims the merciful and saves them from what they deserve, mercy prevents justice from being done. But this does not rob justice, since teaching people to find mercy was the ultimate reason for establishing a system of justice in the first place. If the condition of repentance (that is, of our becoming merciful) has not been realized, however, then it would destroy justice for God to show us mercy, for then mercy would be rescuing people who had not achieved the purposes of justice.

section d: the three moments of mercy

To sum up Alma's account of mercy and justice, let's come back to the apparent incompatibility between justice and mercy. Amulek seems to envision a three-stage dialogue between justice and mercy. First, mercy overpowers justices and disables it. Second, this action on mercy's part "bringeth about means unto men that they may have faith unto repentance" (Alma 34:15). Third, if we take advantage of these means and repent, then "mercy can satisfy the demands of justice, and encircles

[us] in the arms of safety"; otherwise, mercy withdraws her protection, and the person who "exercises no faith unto repentance is exposed to the whole law of the demands of justice" (verse 16). This three-stage process maps on to the different forms of mercy Alma experienced and shows how closely they are intertwined with one another. We said previously that God shows us

1. mercy in giving us time—he delays or postpones justice (see Alma 12:24),
2. mercy in preaching the word—he continues to warn us and through his example teaches us how to exercise faith; (see verses 28–29)
3. the mercy of salvation—he saves us from our just punishment.

The first moment of mercy involves merciful acts that are most directly in conflict with justice because they prevent or at least delay its exercise. God uses that delay to warn us of the punishment that is coming and to show us how to avoid the punishment. These are acts of mercy in the formal sense. God had two options, either of which he could do. He could punish us immediately when we do wrong. Or he could give us a chance to learn from our mistakes and mitigate the damage we have done. The second option is the merciful one. Thus:

there was a time granted unto man to repent, yea, a probationary time, a time to repent and serve God (Alma 42:4).

We called this type of mercy "temporalizing mercy" because it opens up a period of time within which repentance is still possible. It is to this temporalizing mercy that we will turn in Part III.

The first two moments of mercy strain justice by delaying it. The third moment of mercy would destroy justice unless we have repented and experienced a transformation—a changing of our hearts and dispositions that makes us a new creature. But since "the whole meaning of the law" is to point us to Christ's sacrifice, and since the intent of Christ's sacrifice is to "bring about the bowels of mercy" (Alma 34:14–15), the third moment of mercy actually realizes the purpose of justice—but only as long as we repent and become merciful ourselves.

This is emphatically not to say that the repentant sinner no longer deserves a just punishment. Often the wrongs we do cannot be undone. It is in those cases that the power of mercy is most keenly felt. And thus, for the work of making us merciful, the tension between justice and mercy is not something that can or should be dispelled. Take the case of Alma and his companions:

> Now they were desirous that salvation should be declared to every creature, for they could not bear that any human soul should perish; yea, even the very thoughts that any soul should endure endless torment did cause them to quake and tremble. And thus did the Spirit of the Lord work upon them, for they were the very vilest of sinners. And the Lord saw fit in his infinite mercy to spare them; *nevertheless they suffered much anguish of soul because of their iniquities, suffering much and fearing that they should be cast off forever* (Mosiah 28:3–4; emphasis supplied).

Alma and the sons of Helaman never got over the feeling that they justly deserved punishment. The tension never released. They gave full sway to both the justice and mercy of God, and this kept them in the right practical stance. For the purpose of filling our bowels with mercy, the tension between justice and mercy is not something that can or should be dispelled. What tends to make us merciful to others is our awareness of our own need for mercy – that is, when we see that we rightly deserve punishment, but nevertheless have received a merciful gift of forgiveness.

Alma on the Temporal Nature of Human Existence

In Part II, we defined a state of justice as a situation in which each individual has what he or she deserves. And we defined a just act as an action in which one is motivated by a desire to produce a state of justice. But we left the discussion of justice in these very general terms; we did not set out in any detail the character of God's justice. Exactly what does God give us when he gives us what we deserve? That question is the theme of this third part.

As we will see, God's justice is intimately tied up with what we called God's temporalizing mercy—the merciful act of postponing justice in order to give us a space of time to repent. In chapter 8, we will look at Alma's account of the temporal nature of human existence—a temporal nature that is part and parcel of our fallen state. For Alma, the temporal horizon of the future is organized around two events—the resurrection and the judgment. But for Alma, these are not events that will happen later in some distant time. Instead, if God's justice is properly understood, the future constantly informs the meaning of our day-to-day lives now.

The doctrine of restoration is the key to understanding the resurrection, and the resurrection is the key to understanding the justice of God. Accordingly, in chapter 9, we'll look at Alma's account of restoration and resurrection. In chapter 10, we'll look at God's exercise of justice. Is it injustice to consign the sinner to a state of misery? Alma's answer is no, not if it is a state of one's own choosing. Alma teaches us that God's justice involves restoring us to the person we have made ourselves into during the time of our probation—but with one important qualification or restriction. As Lehi noted, all humans are free "to act for themselves and not to be acted upon, save it be by the punishment of the law at the great and last day" (2 Ne. 2:26).

The punishment thus consists in God no longer permitting us to act without constraint. He will no longer allow us to do wrong. For those who are inclined toward doing wrong, who distract themselves from the misery of their condition by harming others, this will be experienced as the wrath of God.

So, the future judgment of God restores spirits to a condition in which the whole being continues to be what he or she is and has been—this insight rounds out Alma's description of human existence. It also confirms why faith and mercy are at the heart of religious life—faith, as a practical stance of active loyalty to God, and mercy, as a characteristic disposition of that practical stance, are acquired (like any skill) through exercise and practice. The person who experiences and responds to this world mercifully is also the person who contributes to the work of redeeming all of human kind and thus is best prepared for eternal life.

8

Death and Probationary Time

In teaching his son Corianton about the fall of Eve and Adam, Alma says something strikingly paradoxical:

> There was a time granted unto man to repent....
> For behold, if Adam had put forth his hand immediately, and partaken of the tree of life, he would have lived forever, according to the word of God, having no space for repentance (Alma 42:4–5).

If Alma is right, this is an extreme case of "more is less": an eternity of time leaves you no time to repent! Why does Alma think this?

On this matter (as on so many others in the Book of Mormon), Lehi is probably the original source. In explaining the fall of Eve and Adam to his own son, Jacob, Lehi offered an important clarification of the account in Genesis. Why exactly was God so anxious to keep Eve and Adam from the fruit of the tree of life (see Gen. 3:22–24)? In the Old Testament the answer is unclear. Many readers infer that depriving humankind of the fruit of the tree of life is part of humankind's punishment for transgressing God's command. Milton, for example, argued that "this bodily death should really be thought of as a punishment for sin."[1] This is not an unreasonable conclusion to draw, given the context. God first curses the serpent "above every beast of the field" (Gen. 3:14). He "greatly multipl[ies]" the woman's "sorrow" (verse 16). He "curses the ground" and condemns the man to hard labor and death (verse 17). Given this series of curses, it is easy to conclude that barring the way to the tree of life (verse 24) is also meant to punish Eve and Adam—indeed, is the climactic punishment. God's primary motivation, it seems, is to ensure that Adam suffers fear and anxiety in the fact of death as a retribution for his sin.

But Lehi's interpretation is different. The fruit of the tree of life and the forbidden fruit of the knowledge of good and evil exist "in opposition. . . the one being sweet and the other bitter" (2 Ne. 2:15). Had humankind not chosen the forbidden fruit, "all things which were created must have remained in the same state which they were, after that they were created; and they must have remained forever, and had no end" (verse 22). The word *end* can mean either "cessation" or "purpose."[2] In this passage, it surely means both. If humankind had elected eternal life in a state of Edenic innocence, they could have existed that way endlessly. But they would have for that very reason lost all sense of purpose. Indeed, Lehi insists that without the opposition of good and bad, of holiness and misery, of wickedness and righteousness, the world "must needs have been created for a thing of naught, wherefore *there would have been no purpose* in the end of its creation" (verse 12; emphasis supplied).

Thus, while fallen humankind longs for eternal life, the fruit of the tree of life is barred to them because fallen humankind needs to change. It is in this way that Lehi sets the stage for Alma's thinking about God's judgment. On Lehi's interpretation of Genesis 3, when God bars the way to the tree of life he does so to preserve for us our capacity for change. Alma expands on this doctrine during his mission to Ammonihah: "If it were possible that our first parents could have gone forth and partaken of the tree of life they would have been forever miserable, having no preparatory state" (Alma 12:26). But once "death comes upon mankind," they gain a purpose: "to prepare to meet God" and "to prepare for that endless state which has been spoken of by us, which is after the resurrection of the dead" (verse 24). Once humankind has fallen, the fruit of the tree of life becomes a terrible danger because humankind cannot afford any longer to "remain in the same state which they were." Thus, death is not part of human-kind's punishment. The capacity to change and the death that comes with it are rather manifestations of God's mercy.

Change takes time. It takes repetitive work and training to acquire a new practical stance—a new way of seeing and feeling and being disposed to respond to the world. To overcome our fallen, selfish natures, we need lots of practice. Besides the gift of temporal death, then, God provides a further act of mercy:

> The days of children of men were prolonged, according to the will of God, that they might repent while in the flesh; wherefore, their state became a state of probation, and their time was lengthened, according to the commandments which the Lord God gave unto the children of men. For he gave commandment that all men must repent. (2 Ne. 2:21)

Amulek sums this doctrine up nicely in his sermon to the Zoramites:

> Behold, this life is the time for men to prepare to meet God; yea, behold the day of this life is the day for men to perform their labors.... Do not procrastinate the day of your repentance until the end; for after this day of life, which is given us to prepare for eternity, behold, if we do not improve our time while in this life, then cometh the night of darkness wherein there can be no labor performed. (Alma 34:32–33)

116

This brings us back to Alma's contribution to the doctrine of the fall. Alma recognizes that forever is too much time to give urgency and meaning to the need to change. Therefore, Alma argues, "it was appointed unto man to die" (Alma 42:6). And, he adds, "it was not expedient that man should be reclaimed from this temporal death, for that would destroy the great plan of happiness" (verse 8). Salvation from temporal death, in other words, would not advance us toward the ultimate end and purpose of existence. At first glance, this might seem confusing. Don't we believe that we all will eventually be redeemed from death (see Hel. 14:16)—indeed, that being redeemed from death is expedient to the great plan of happiness? So why would Alma say this? The answer is that there is a difference between *reclaiming* and *redeeming*. Redeeming from death occurs after death. We are hostages to death, but we are purchased or liberated from it once it has occurred. Reclaiming us from death, on the other hand, would occur before death. It would mean calling death off, bringing us back from a condition in which we are prone to death. Our "temporal death," Alma teaches, means that we have fallen into a finite temporality. We die a temporal death because our life is bounded and subject to change. It would not be expedient to be reclaimed from temporal existence because that existence is what enables us to work to transform our fallen nature. A limited time frame gives us focus and a purpose. The finitude of existence provides the context within which our actions show up as having extra weight.

To illustrate this, imagine a fantastical game called "never-ending basketball." The rules of never-ending basketball are exactly like the rules of regular basketball—with two exceptions. There is no clock and players can never foul out (or otherwise be expelled from the game). The game, once started, will never stop. For the avid basketball player or fan, this might initially seem like the ultimate basketball match. But even a moment's reflection will show that it is the opposite. In never-ending basketball, no event matters at all. Suppose that one team quickly runs up a two-hundred-point lead. In normal basketball, this would be a disaster of unprecedented proportions for the other team. But it is a razor-thin lead in never-ending basketball, given that a reasonably diligent team might expect to score tens of thousands of points in the next year alone, never mind the millions of points they could score in the next century. It is the boundedness of normal basketball that makes the points matter.

Similarly, Alma suggests that it is the limited time frame of mortal existence that makes what we do in this life matter. Thus, it is "not expedient that man should be reclaimed from this temporal death" because mortal life "became a preparatory state" as a result of the inevitable and unsurpassable reality of death. (Alma 42:9–10)

For what are we meant to prepare during our finite span of temporal life? The judgment, of course (we'll look at that in chapter 10), but the judgment is just the gateway to a life without the kind of temporal boundaries that characterize our mortal existence. We need to learn to live a life that matters even without a time clock. And that, I would suggest, requires us to recognize and organize our lives around things and people that intrinsically bear infinite and eternal weight. In his early ministry to the people of Zarahemla, Alma set out three main features of people who are prepared for eternity: they are humble, they are contented, they are charitable and kind (see Alma 5:28–31).

9

Death and Restoration

Chapters 39 through 42 of the book of Alma are jointly
entitled "The Commandments of Alma, to his son
Corianton."[1] However, most of these chapters are
taken up not with commandments but with a series
of extended meditations on questions that "worried"
Corianton. These worries center on the resurrection of
the dead (chapter 40), the restoration that coincides
with that resurrection (chapter 41), and the justice of
God in the punishment of sinners (chapter 42). Alma
makes it clear that these concepts—resurrection, restoration, and judgment—are all closely interconnected.
Alma teaches Corianton that God's justice—including
both the reward for the righteous and the just punishment of sinners—simply consists in the restoration to
each one of us what is proper to her or him. This restoration, in turn, simply is the resurrection. In this chapter, we'll set out the basic parameters of Alma's account
of resurrection and restoration. In the next chapter,
we'll explore at last the character of God's justice.

section a: two deaths
God warned Eve and Adam in the garden that to choose
knowledge of good and evil meant certain death: "In
the day that thou eatest thereof thou shalt surely die"
(Gen. 2:17; see also Alma 12:23). The serpent contra-
dicted God: "Ye shall not surely die: For God doth know
that in the day ye eat thereof, then your eyes shall be
opened, and ye shall be as gods, knowing good and
evil" (Gen. 3:4–5). On a common understanding of

death—in which it means something like "altogether ceasing to exist"—it looks like the serpent was the more accurate prognosticator. But Alma teaches that Eve, Adam, and their children are not the kind of beings that can altogether cease to exist: "The soul could never die" (Alma 42:9). So *death* cannot mean what it does in the common understanding.

Alma instead defines death in general as a condition of being "cut off" (see, e.g., Alma 42:9, 9:11). This is not a mere metaphor: to be "cut off" from something means to be unable to engage with it, respond to it, influence it, or be influenced by it. As a consequence of the fallenness of humankind, we are all "cut off from the tree of life" and thus we shall "be cut off from the face of the earth" (Alma 42:6)—where being cut off from the earth means being unable to take part in the activities of earthly existence. We are also "cut off both temporally and spiritually from the presence of the Lord" (verse 7). That is the kind of death that Eve and Adam suffered in the very day that they ate the forbidden fruit. To be cut off temporally means to belong to a different temporal order than God does. As we discussed in the previous chapter, our existence is bounded by birth and death. Because of our mortality, spans of times matter to us. To God, when exactly some particular event happens "mattereth not; all is as one day with God, and time only is measured unto men" (Alma 40:8).[2] To be cut off spiritually means that fallen humankind has a different way of caring about things than God does. Fallen beings do not see and respond to the same meanings that God does—for instance, they put far more stock in selfish pleasures and satisfaction of desires than God does.

Mortal life is a kind of death. We are dying from the moment we are born, wearing ourselves away as we proceed inexorably toward the grave (when we will no longer be able to engage with the world). But we are not just on the way to death—to being cut off from earthly activities. We are also cut off from God, living without the ultimate source of life. "They are without God in the world," Alma notes, "and they have gone contrary to the nature of God; therefore, they are in a state contrary to the nature of happiness" (Alma 41:11). Alma describes this fallen human existence as a kind of living death. When Eve and Adam came to know good and evil, the first evil that they experienced was shame before God. In hiding themselves from the good, they knew evil. Fallen humankind is this paradox of wanting life (the good) and being unable to live in the fullest sense because we have cut ourselves off from the source of life. In the day they ate of the tree of the knowledge of good and evil, Eve and Adam died because they were cut off from God both temporally and spiritually (see Gen. 2:17). God, not the serpent, had it right after all.[3] In setting temporal death as a limit to this living spiritual death—in barring the way to the tree of life—God assured us that this present existence, this living death, would die. He gave us the merciful gift of the possibility of the death of spiritual death.

section b: resurrection

Alma notes that Corianton's "mind is worried concerning the resurrection of the dead" (Alma 40:1). We are not told precisely what the nature of these worries are. But from Alma's response, we can surmise that they are centered on uncertainty about the precise nature and timing of the resurrection. Is the resurrected soul embodied? Does it happen immediately after death, or is there a delay between death and resurrection? If there is a delay, what happens to the soul between death and resurrection? Is our basic character or nature changed after the resurrection? To many people in the modern

Church, the answer to these questions is obvious. But that is only because Alma lays out his doctrine with a clarity and precision that is not matched in other scriptural accounts of the resurrection. Let's look at Alma's answer to each question in turn.

Is the resurrected soul embodied? Resurrection literally means to rise up again to a higher level—"the raising of the spirit or the soul," as Alma puts it (Alma 40:15). The Old Testament taught that after death "shall the dust return to the earth as it was: and the spirit shall return unto God who gave it" (Eccl. 12:7). Alma confirmed that "the spirits of all men, as soon as they are departed from this mortal body, yea, the spirits of all men, whether they be good or evil, are taken home to that God who gave them life" (Alma 40:11).

Abinadi taught that there is a distinction between a first and a subsequent resurrection (see Mosiah 15:20–21).[4] The doctrine of the first resurrection was incorporated into the baptismal covenant taught by Alma's father. Members of the church of God covenanted "to mourn with those that mourn; yea, and comfort those that stand in need of comfort, and to stand as witnesses of God at all times and in all things, and in all places." In return, they received a promise that they would "be redeemed of God, and be numbered with those of the first resurrection." (Mosiah 18:9)

In the church in Alma's day, some had apparently understood the first resurrection as the postmortem return of the spirit to God. Alma concedes that, given the literal meaning of the word *resurrection*, the "raising of the spirit or the soul" could be called a resurrection: "Yea, I admit it may be termed a resurrection" (Alma 40:15). But, he clarified, this was not the resurrection promised to us by God (see verses 17–18).

In all of scripture, only Amulek (see Alma 11:45) affirms as clearly as Alma does that the resurrection involves a reunification of spirit and body: "It is requisite and just, according to the power and resurrection of Christ, that the soul of man should be restored to its body, and that every part of the body should be restored to itself" (Alma 41:2).

When is the resurrection? Alma's short answer is: "No one knows; but God knoweth the time which is appointed" (Alma 40:4). Alma does know that it will not be "until after the coming of Christ" because "he bringeth to pass the resurrection of the dead" (verses 2–3). Alma affirms the universal character of the resurrection—"there is a time appointed that *all* shall rise from the dead" (verse 5; emphasis supplied)—although this does not mean that all will be resurrected at the same time: "Whether there shall be one time, or a second time, or a third time, that men shall come forth from the dead, it mattereth not; for God knoweth all these things" (verse 5).

What happens to the soul between death and resurrection? Alma asserts that "there must needs be a space betwixt the time of death and the time of the resurrection" (verse 6). While he doesn't explain why there needs to be such a space, he does discuss that state of the soul during this time. Here again, Alma offers one of the most detailed discussions on the postmortem state of the soul that is found anywhere in scripture.

The lack of biblical clarity on this issue has led to centuries of theological debates over whether Christianity is committed to an immortal soul that survives death and awaits resurrection or whether the soul and body both perish at death and are annihilated until the complete human being is resurrected. For instance, John Milton argued that "the whole man dies," meaning "each separate part"—spirit and body—"dies."[5] "For those who have died," Milton posits, "all intervening time will be as nothing, so that to them it will seem that they die and are with Christ at the same moment."[6] "What could be more absurd," Milton reasoned,

> than that the part which sinned most (i.e., the soul), should escape the sentence of death; or that the body, which was just as immortal as the soul before sin brought death into the world, should alone pay the penalty for sin by dying although it had no actual part in the sin?[7]

Philosophers worry, however, that if the whole soul—body and spirit—is annihilated at any point, then the resurrected being is not genuinely the same identical person as the one who died. The resurrected being is a replica, not the original. A theory that avoids this problem is one (sometimes but not consistently) espoused by Martin Luther, who was of the view that "the dead are completely asleep and do not feel anything at all. The dead lie there without counting days or years; but when they are raised, it will seem to them that they have only slept for a moment."[8]

Alma, by contrast, declares that "the state of the soul between death and the resurrection . . . has been made known unto me by an angel" (Alma 40:11).[9] "The soul," Alma teaches, "could never die" (Alma 42:9). Consequently, the state of humankind after death is one of dissolution into parts. The body has perished, but "the spirits of all men, whether they be good or evil," continue to exist and "are taken home to that God who gave them life" (Alma 40:11). Nor are they in a state of sleep. Rather, Alma reveals, "the spirits of those who are righteous are received into a state of happiness, which is called paradise, a state of rest, a state of peace, where they shall rest from all their troubles and from all care, and sorrow" (verse 12). "The souls of the wicked," on the other hand, are in a state of "darkness, and a state of awful, fearful looking for the fiery indignation of the wrath of God upon them; thus they remain in this state, as well as the righteous in paradise, until the time of their resurrection" (verse 14). As we'll see in the next chapter, this anxiety on the part of the wicked appears to be largely of their own making. Alma does not describe the judgment as the fiery and indignant and wrathful punishment exercised on the wicked. That the wicked fear a terrible revenge perhaps tells us more about their way of treating others than it does about God.

Does the resurrection change our basic character or nature? Alma teaches that the resurrection is a restoration, not a transformation (verses 21–22). At the resurrection we receive incorruptible bodies and are no longer prone to temporal death (Alma 41:4). But our basic character or nature is unchanged—we are restored in such a way that we will still be the same individual we once were, having the same body, inclinations, tendencies, and desires we had in mortal life:

> The soul shall be restored to the body, and the body to the soul; yea, and every limb and joint shall be restored to its body; yea, even a hair of the head shall not be lost; but all things shall be restored to their proper and perfect frame (Alma 40:23).

A frame is an ordered arrangement of connected parts. Thus, the body is a frame—it is made up of organs and limbs that are organized to facilitate life. The human being as a whole is a frame—it is made up of the body and spirit, joined and mutually influencing one another, in such a way as to organize a distinctively human form of existence. At death, these frames (of the body, and of the whole human being) are broken up and dissolved.

The resurrection is just the restoration of these frames to their order, but with an important qualification. The restoration will bring them into a perfect frame—that is, into the finished or consummate form of that organization. So the defects in our bodies, or in the spirit's integration with the body, will be removed. This qualification has its own qualification: the perfection of the frame will not be such as to erase our individuality. The resurrection will restore each of us to our proper frame. In the American English usage of the time in which the Book of Mormon was translated, the primary meaning of *proper* was to denote what is distinctive of or peculiar to a particular individual, what he or she is particularly fitted to.[10] The opposite of *proper* would be *generic*. Thus a "proper name," for instance, belongs to one specific individual. My "proper frame" or "proper order" is the organization of my parts so that I can function in my own distinctive way.

When Alma says "the plan of restoration is requisite with the justice of God," he explains that this is because "it is requisite that all things should be restored to their proper order" (Alma 41:2). That is necessary because the justice of God involves my receiving the reward or punishment that I deserve in virtue of the particular individual who I am. It would be unjust if I were rewarded or punished after being resurrected into a state that is distinct from who I was in life, for then I would no longer be the individual who merited that punishment or reward.

Thus, the restoration will return people to a condition that allows them to resume being the people that they have made themselves into during their lives. In this way, the concept of restoration bridges the gap between resurrection and judgment. One could say that, for Alma, the resurrection is just a restoration, and a restoration is just the judgment of God:

> All things shall be restored to their proper order, every thing to its natural frame..., the one raised to happiness according to his

desires of happiness, or good according to his desires of good; and the other to evil according to his desires of evil; for as he has desired to do evil all the day long even so shall he have his reward of evil when the night cometh (Alma 41:4–5).

The implication of the doctrine of restoration is this: God's judgment on us consists in restoring to us the dispositions we develop over a lifetime. Hence, when we perform a bad action, there is a need to repent (i.e., to change course), for such an action repeated often enough will grow into a disposition to do wrong.

10

Judgment

In Part II, we explored Alma's claim that the end or the purpose of the law is to make us merciful. Our becoming merciful (i.e., repenting) is the condition on which mercy can overpower justice and claim us as her own. We also saw that mercy is experienced most powerfully in those cases where punishment is deserved. If the punishment is undeserved, then it is not an act of mercy on God's part to forego the punishment; it is an act of justice. So for a complete understanding of Alma's doctrine—a doctrine which sees justice and mercy as standing in a productive tension with each other—we need to show that God's judgments are in fact fundamentally just.

Alma takes up the question of the justice of God's judgment in the context of responding to his son Corianton's worried state of mind:

> My son, I perceive there is somewhat more which doth worry your mind, which ye cannot understand—which is concerning the justice of God in the punishment of the sinner; for ye do try to suppose that it is injustice that the sinner should be consigned to a state of misery (Alma 42:1).

We don't have the full story here—we don't know why Corianton believes there is injustice in punishing sinners. Perhaps he is worried about the disproportion between temporal harms and eternal misery. If we understand the eternal as endless in duration, it does seem fundamentally unfair to punish temporal and finite crimes—no matter how awful—with a never-ending suffering. As we noted in chapter 5, however, God's eternal or endless punishment does not necessarily mean that it lasts interminably. Alma's own eternal torment lasted for only three days (Alma 36:12). When Alma describes something as "eternal" or "endless," he means that its character is not diminished by the passage of time—not that it actually does exist forever, in other words, but that it could exist forever without changing in any essential respect. An eternal punishment is one that no person could get used to. It would be just as miserable on the third or the three millionth day as it was on the first. But that it could last forever does not mean that it does last forever. Thus, God's punishments can be both eternal and strictly proportional to the wrong done.

Judging by the thrust of Alma's response, however, it is likely that Corianton has a different concern. Alma's response is almost entirely preoccupied with demonstrating that the suffering the wicked experience following God's judgment is something that flows immediately and directly and naturally from their actions. It is likely, therefore, that Corianton's worries are a result of his failure to understand this doctrine. Corianton is not alone in this respect. Many people have a "coercive" view of punishment—that is, a view that punishment is a means to coerce people into doing something that is extrinsic to their wishes or desires. If we think it is appropriate to punish someone to deter them from doing what they want to do, for example, we hold a coercive view of punishment. One could conceivably justify a coercive use of punishment by showing ① that the end being pursued through coercion is a good end, ② that there is no better way to achieve the end, and ③ that the pain inflicted by the punishment is outweighed by the good achieved through the use of coercion. But uncertainty about each of these justifications can give rise to worries about the justice of the coercive use of punishment. And there is an enduring worry whether coercing a person is itself bad (no matter how good the end is), because coercion fails to respect that person's dignity as a free agent.

Alma's response to Corianton does not address any of these worries. Instead, Alma offers an alternative, noncoercive view of punishment. In Alma's view, God's punishment consists in allowing me to experience the consequences of being the person into whom I have made myself through my choices. By allowing me to experience the suffering that comes from having a bad character, God helps me to understand the significance of what I have done. But he leaves it up to me to decide what I want to do about it. The punishment is thus part and parcel of helping us grow as agents. It brings us to understand how wrongdoing cuts us off from the good and encourages us to overcome our alienation from God and our fellow beings.

We laid out in the previous chapter the basic framework within which Alma develops his account of the justice of God. The question of God's justice is for Alma intimately tied up with the resurrection and restoration of our bodies and spirits to their proper and perfect frame. "The plan of restoration," Alma teaches, "is requisite with the justice of God; for it is requisite that all things should be restored to their proper order" (Alma 41:2). Let's tease out the implications of this insight.

section a: restoration and justice
In chapter 7 we defined a state of justice as a situation or condition in which each individual has what he or she deserves. What, exactly, do I deserve? Alma's proposal is that I deserve my "proper order." This means that I

deserve to be allowed to function in my own distinctive way. That thought gets coupled in Alma's teaching with a second insight—namely, that an internal relation exists between happiness and righteousness/goodness. By an *internal relation*, I mean that happiness flows naturally from righteousness or goodness. Similarly, Alma argues that an internal relationship exists between misery and wickedness. This is evident when, for example, Alma instructs Corianton that

> all men that are in a state of nature, or I would say, in a carnal state, are in the gall of bitterness and in the bonds of iniquity; they are without God in the world, and they have gone contrary to the nature of God; therefore, *they are in a state contrary to the nature of happiness* (Alma 41:11; emphasis supplied).

To be carnally minded, self-absorbed and focused exclusively on immediate pleasures—that is intrinsically to be in "the gall of bitterness" (in other words, to be intensely resentful and sorrowful). To put the point a little differently, we could say that it is in the nature of happiness that it can be experienced only by the righteous. Likewise, it is in the nature of wickedness that it entails misery and sorrow. Thus, when the resurrection restores "every thing to its natural frame," this has the consequence of "raising us" either "to endless happiness . . . or to endless misery" (verse 4).

So we can now give our earlier, formal definition of a state of justice some content, restating it thus:

> Justice is a condition in which the righteous are happy and the wicked are miserable.

But it is a feature of our fallen world that this condition does not obtain universally. The wicked are often the most adept at supplying themselves with pleasures that mask their misery, even if they cannot quite extinguish it. Meanwhile the righteous are as prone as anyone to deep sorrow, disease, intense suffering, and death. It is this lack of justice that the law is designed to correct.

section b: the law

The righteous, although intrinsically deserving of happiness, are all too often deprived of this happiness by others' bad behavior. But one might worry that the fact that we live in a fallen world in and of itself makes God's judgment fundamentally unjust. The problem is this: in a world in which the wicked prosper and enjoy pleasures while the righteous suffer, it is hard to recognize the form of life that will, in the long run, allow us to experience happiness. To ameliorate that problem, God gives us the law. Alma identifies three ways in which the law alters our situation. When a "just law" has "a punishment affixed," Alma says, it

① gives justice and mercy "a claim upon the creature" (Alma 42:21),
② "br[ings] remorse of conscience unto man" (verse 18), and
③ makes us "afraid to sin" (verse 20).

Let's look at each of these in turn.

One fundamental precondition on a judgment being just is that the law itself, when followed, improves the overall condition of society. By publicly articulating and enforcing rules that (when followed) get everyone to approximate a good life, the laws put us on notice that we will be held accountable for our success or failure in trying to live that life. As Alma puts it, justice then has a "claim" on us—it can rightfully demand something of us. A second fundamental precondition is that the law gives us advance notice of the punishment or mercy that our behavior will incur. Jacob taught that "where there is no law given there is no punishment; and where there is no punishment there is no condemnation"

(2 Ne. 9:25). There are a couple of ways in which the law puts us on notice of its just demands.

The threat of punishment motivates us to follow the law. When we live according to the law, it trains our dispositions in such a way that the prospect (or recollection) of breaking the law awakens a sharp sense of guilt or anguish. This feeling of a sharp, biting, regret or guilt is what Alma means by "the remorse of conscience."[1] So the law plays an essential role in teaching us to distinguish between good and bad.

Christ is the perfect exemplar of a way of living that would produce a world where goodness and happiness coincide. The law points us to a Christlike way to live. In the language of the Book of Mormon, the law is "the typifying of [Christ]" (2 Ne. 11:4). The word *typify* is ambiguous between two related but distinct concepts. It can mean, on the one hand, "to represent or express [something] by a type or symbol"; "to symbolize; to prefigure."[2] A type in this sense is "that by which something is symbolized or figured."[3] For instance, the Israelite sacrifice of a goat as a sin offering was taken in the Book of Mormon (and in Christianity more generally) as a type or symbol of the atoning sacrifice of Christ (see Lev. 4:24; 9:15). But this kind of symbolical typifying can explain only a fraction of the law of Moses, and it doesn't even touch the most morally significant parts of the law (such as the ten commandments). And yet Amulek teaches that "every whit" of the law, and not just the ritualistic parts, "[points] to the Son of God" (Alma 34:14).

There is another meaning to the word *type* that can do justice to Amulek's claim. A *type* is not just a symbol of something. It can also refer to "the general form, structure, or character distinguishing a particular kind, group, or class of beings or objects." A type in this sense is a "thing that exemplifies the ideal qualities or characteristics of a kind"; it is "a perfect example or specimen of something."[4] Thus one thing typifies another when it "exhibit[s] the essential characters" of that kind of thing. If we think of the law as typifying Christ in this way, then we can do justice to Amulek's claim that "the whole meaning of the law" points to "the Son of God" (Alma 34:14). The moral commandments and teachings of the law typify or are a type of Christ because they show us the essential qualities and the characteristics that distinguish Christ. Christ, in turn, is the model or exemplar of the righteous life—the kind of life that, if lived by all, would result in a world where the righteous enjoy happiness. The law is fulfilled in Christ because he perfectly embodies the kind of life envisioned by the moral teachings of the law. Once Christ has shown us in the flesh how we ought to live, we no longer need a symbolic representation of him. Thus the sacrifices and other symbolic aspects of the law of Moses can drop away. But the moral aspects of the law continue to have a hold on us because they continue to offer us guidance as we pattern our lives on Christ.

So the law typifies Christ. And in submitting to the law, one's practical stance is trained so that we come to feel intense guilt and anguish at the prospect of violating the law. In this way, the law disposes us to behave in a way which, if universally adhered to, would result in a world where happiness more perfectly coincides with righteousness.

The law also helps create a world in which the good—those who are capable of and worthy of happiness—are the ones who in fact enjoy happiness. It does this by disciplining those who act badly, thus discouraging wickedness more generally. It is important to state this point carefully. In Alma's view, wickedness is in itself a kind of misery. All it takes for the wicked to recognize and directly experience their misery is to deprive them of the carnal pleasures and worldly activities they use to anaesthetize themselves. Alma observes of the wicked that "as soon as they were dead their souls were miserable" (Alma 42:11). Alma knows this firsthand; in his confrontation with the angel, once he was no longer able to distract himself with worldly activities and pleasures and concerns, he found himself "in the gall of bitterness, and . . . encircled about by the everlasting chains of death" (Alma 36:18). Happiness cannot be experienced by someone in that state. This is why "wickedness never was happiness" (Alma 41:10). Thus it is simply not possible, even for God, to restore someone "from sin to happiness" (verse 10). Misery is intrinsically "affixed" to wickedness.

Thus in the proper order of things—the one that will obtain after the final judgment—no extra punishment will need to be inflicted on the wicked. The ultimate punishment for wickedness, according to the principle of restoration, is that each wicked individual has to be the miserable person that he or she has become. The final punishment is spiritual death, as the wicked cut themselves off from the ocean of love they would share in fellowship with the righteous who live in God's presence (see Alma 40:26). But in the meantime, temporal punishments can be attached to earthly laws in an attempt to move us closer to a world in which justice prevails, the good are happy, and the wicked are miserable. Temporal punishments do this by imposing suffering on the wicked to awaken a sense of fear in them.

section c: the justice of God's judgments
With all of this in view, it is a relatively straightforward matter to demonstrate that God's judgments are in fact just. By typifying Christ, the law has shown us what the good life is. It has put us on notice of the wrongfulness of bad behavior. It has given us a start toward developing correct practices and shaping our dispositions

and emotional responses to the world. It is in the light of our understanding of good and evil that we spend our probation forming our characters. God's final judgment consists in resurrecting us—that is, restoring to us the good or evil work that we have done in forming our character (see Alma 41:3–4). It is only in the resurrected state that righteousness coincides perfectly with happiness:

> Therefore, all things shall be restored to their proper order, every thing to its natural frame—mortality raised to immortality, corruption to incorruption—...the one restored to happiness according to his desires of happiness, or to good according to his desires of good; and the other to evil according to his desires of evil; for as he has desired to do evil all the day long even so shall he have his reward of evil when the night cometh (verses 4–5).[5]

Thus Alma suggests that the perfect coincidence of righteousness and happiness on the one hand, and the perfect coincidence of wickedness and misery on the other hand, is part of the proper order and natural frame of things—a proper order that can be realized only in the resurrection.

But it also follows that human beings "are their own judges" because they decide for themselves "whether to do good or do evil" (verse 7). The wicked can thus hardly complain when God restores to them the fruits of their wickedness—that is, their bad character and dispositions. As a result of who they are, they will continue longing for wickedness but without the compensatory pleasures that flow to the wicked in a fallen word. In other words, God will not allow them to continue performing acts of wickedness.

The reward of righteousness is, first and foremost, the restoration to the righteous of the fruits of righteousness—namely, a good character and good dispositions. The character and dispositions they have developed—humility, receptivity to the needs of others and mercy and a desire to forgive—will allow them to enjoy the society of the good.

Epilogue

Given Alma's overriding interest in practice rather than theory, what can I hope to have achieved with a "theological introduction" to the book of Alma? I would count this little book a success if it sent you back to the words of Alma with an open heart, more susceptible than before to the challenges Alma presents to our day and age. After all, familiarity breeds neglect. The more at home I am with something—be it a person, a city, a text—the less I am able to recognize just how remarkable it is, or how little I understand its full richness and complexity. But sharing the familiar with a new companion lets me see the old through a new set of eyes. In the end, it matters little how knowledgeable or perceptive the companion is; that he or she has a different perspective than me is enough for me to see the old anew.

So I wrote in the hope that I could accompany you as you returned to the book of Alma, that my perspective on Alma would prompt you to experience his words afresh. My general perspective is this: Alma's ministry was devoted to attacking background assumptions about the world that distort our relationship to God and to each other. Ironically, the greatest obstacle to understanding Alma's doctrine is the fact that we continue to hold the very assumptions or prejudices he attacks. One of these assumptions is that religious faith is primarily concerned with belief or knowledge—that to stand in the right relationship to God is to believe the right things about God. Another is the idea that I merit or deserve God's mercy as a result of what I do. A third is that God's justice is a form of vengeance.

Alma's experience taught him that these assumptions distort our faith and prevent us from letting Christ's mercy transform our hearts. When we develop a humble, merciful, active loyalty to God, we can experience a joy in being together that will convince us of God's goodness far more effectively than any intellectual proof.

Perhaps the most inspiring aspect of the doctrine developed by Alma and his companions is their conviction that the better world they aspire to is not a fantastical dream. Amulek concludes his address to the Zoramites with a remarkable promise:

> *Now is the time and the day of your salvation*; and therefore, if ye will repent and harden not your hearts, immediately shall the great plan of redemption be brought about unto you. For behold, this life is the time for men to prepare to meet God; yea, behold the day of this life is the day for men to perform their labors. (Alma 34:31–32; emphasis supplied)

The time for redemption is now—in the immediate present. Isn't this the ultimate significance of the doctrine of judgment as restoration—that eternal life in the presence of God is essentially the same as the life we should be living now? The salvation we hope for is found in the day-to-day exercise of faith, as we perform the works of mercy, of kindness, of humility, and of love.

Endnotes

SERIES INTRODUCTION

1. Elder Neal A. Maxwell, "The Children of Christ" (Brigham Young University devotional, Feb. 4, 1990), https://speeches.byu.edu/talks/neal-a-maxwell/children-christ/.

2. Elder Neal A. Maxwell, "The Inexhaustible Gospel" (Brigham Young University devotional, Aug. 18, 1992), https://speeches.byu.edu/talks/neal-a-maxwell/inexhaustible-gospel/.

3. Elder Neal A. Maxwell, "The Book of Mormon: A Great Answer to 'The Great Question'" (address given at the Book of Mormon Symposium, Brigham Young University, Provo, UT, Oct. 10, 1986), reprinted in *The Voice of My Servants: Apostolic Messages on Teaching, Learning, and Scripture,* ed. Scott C. Esplin and Richard Neitzel Holzapfel (Provo, UT: Religious Studies Center, Brigham Young University; Salt Lake City: Deseret Book, 2010), 221–38, https://rsc.byu.edu/archived/voice-my-servants/book-mormon-great-answer-great-question.

PART I

1

1. There are a few passages that speak of "faith in the words" of the prophets—when they're prophesying about Christ. See, for example, Mosiah 26:15–16 or Alma 57:26.

2. See, for example, Alma's discussion of the Liahona: "They were slothful, and forgot to exercise their faith and diligence and then those marvelous works ceased, and they did not progress in their journey" (Alma 37:41).

3. Russell M. Nelson, "The Book of Mormon: What Would Your Life Be Like without It?" *Ensign* or *Liahona*, November 2017, 60–63,

https://www.churchofjesuschrist.org/study/general-confer-ence/2017/10/the-book-of-mormon-what-would-your-life-be-like-without-it?lang=eng.

4. To be more precise, I'd define faith as a practical stance in which

Ⓐ A is loyal to and trusts in God, and

Ⓑ A has dispositions to act that are shaped by that loyalty and trust, and

Ⓒ A actually does act as motivated by those dispositions.

Those dispositions to act typically

① involve perceptual capacities for perceiving the world in the light of God,

② are guided by affective responses (i.e., feelings and moods) that are attuned to the good as ordained by God,

③ are purposively directed at some end ordained by God.

For simplicity's sake, however, I'll use the shorthand definition.

2

1. I have modified the punctuation. See also Alma 30:48.

2. He does ask Alma to intervene on his behalf with God (Alma 30:54). But this is a far cry from genuine repentance.

3. There is good reason to suspect that Korihor's confession is itself a lie. A man whose core ethical principle is that "whatsoever a man did was no crime" is unlikely to feel any compunction about doing whatever it takes to "prosper according to his genius" (Alma 30:17)—including saying what he thinks Alma wants to hear.

4. *American Dictionary of the English Language*, 1st ed. (1828), s.v. "genius," http://webstersdictionary1828.com/Dictionary/genius.

5. Alma insists on this repeatedly: see Alma 36:1, 30; 37:13; 38:1.

3

1. Members of "the poor class of people" were "cast out of the syna-gogues because of the coarseness of their apparel—Therefore they were not permitted to enter into their synagogues to worship God" (Alma 32:2–3).

4

1. See Daniel Becerra, *3rd, 4th Nephi: A Brief Theological Introduction* (Provo, UT: Neal A. Maxwell Institute for Religious Scholarship, 2020).

2. See "Faith," *Children's Songbook* (Salt Lake City, UT: Deseret Book Company, 1991), 96.

3. Remember, the modern division into verses was not part of the original text of the Book of Mormon. When read in the context of the immediately preceding verses, it's clear that *believe* here is an elliptical expression for "believe in." Reading *believe* here as "believe that" makes the sentence false. This is because if I know something, then I certainly do have a cause or motivational impulse toward believing it: I have a surety that it is true. What better cause or motivation could I have for believing it than that? But the relationship between knowledge and belief-in is more complicated. If I believe in the word of God, this means something like the following: I make the word of God the particular object in which I rest my trust or confidence; I surrender my own will to the word of God, and I accept the guidance of the word of God. Knowing that such-and-such is true is not the same as being moved to accept it as my guide. After all, "the devils also believe, and tremble," but they don't accept God's word as authoritative for them (James 2:18–19).

4. *American Dictionary of the English Language*, 1st ed. (1828), s.v. "cause," http://webstersdictionary1828.com/Dictionary/cause.

5. Of course, knowledge is not faith. Reading the question in this way renders it a trivial point and, more importantly, misses the central point of the question: to focus us on what constitutes a faithful case of believing-in.

6. Someone might ask: "What about the passages in Alma that single out knowing transgression for special blame? Isn't Alma contradicting himself here?" (see, e.g., Alma 24:30; 9:23). There is no contradiction because those passages are talking about an additional dimension of wrongdoing that exists when the wrongdoer stands in a personal relationship to the lawgiver. If the lawgiver expressly forbids me to perform some act, and I do perform that act knowing that it has been forbidden, I am guilty of two misdemeanors: first, I am guilty of whatever wrong I performed (and this guilt, as we have seen, doesn't diminish as long as I believe or have cause to believe that it is wrong—no knowledge is necessary here). In addition, I am guilty of open rebellion against the lawgiver. For

instance, if I eat the whole pan of brownies my mother just baked without her permission, I am guilty of gluttony. If, in addition, my mother expressly tells me that she has baked the brownies for our ailing neighbor and asks me not to eat them, I am guilty not just of gluttony but also of damaging my relationship to my mother. In this latter case, my action manifests a heightened form of hardness of heart. This is why Alma teaches that "after a people have been once enlightened by the Spirit of God, and have had great knowledge of things pertaining to righteousness, and then have fallen away into sin and transgression, they become more hardened, and thus their state becomes worse than though they had never known these things" (Alma 24:30; see also Alma 9:23).

7. "Unto . . . indicat[es] a resultant condition, status, or capacity: in or into the character, nature, or quality of." *Oxford English Dictionary,* s.v. "unto," definition 11, https://www.oed.com/view/Entry/218976

8. Alma never says so explicitly, but perhaps he thought (as Jacob did) that perfect knowledge is something we can hope for only after the resurrection (see 2 Ne. 9:13–14). Alma of course believes that, in exceptional cases, a kind of direct knowledge is possible—a belief that God exists that is secured by direct experience of God (see Alma 36:26). But there is no indication that this kind of knowledge is something to which we can reasonably aspire.

9. The book of Alma was originally divided into thirty chapters. Chapter 16 comprises the encounter with Korihor (modern chapter 30), the initial encounter with the Zoramites (chapter 31), the Sermon on the Seed (chapters 32 and 33), Amulek's sermon on the Christ (chapter 34), and a narrative conclusion of the mission to the Zoramites (chapter 35).

10. See Royal Skousen, "How Joseph Smith Translated the Book of Mormon: Evidence from the Original Manuscript," *Journal of Book of Mormon Studies* 7 (1998): 27–28.

11. I follow Royal Skousen's restoration of the "and" to verse 35. See Skousen, ed. *Analysis of Textual Variants of the Book of Mormon, Part 4,* Critical Text of the Book of Mormon 4 (Provo, UT: Foundation for Ancient Research and Mormon Studies [FARMS], 2014), 2232; also available at https://interpreterfoundation.org/books/atv/p4/.

12. He died—could it be a coincidence?—after being trampled while begging house to house among the Zoramites (Alma 31:58–59). Perhaps this reveals that Zoramite attacks on the poor were more than merely rhetorical in nature. We do know that the poor were literally "cast out" of their synagogues (see Alma 32:2, 5, 9).

1. This is Korihor's version of the objection. The Zoramite version is found in Alma 31:16–17.

2. *American Dictionary of the English Language*, 1st ed. (1828), s.v. "whit," accessed September 18, 2020, http://webstersdictionary1828.com/Dictionary/whit.

5

1. Of course, credal trinitarianism attempts to rationalize this teaching by, for instance, invoking philosophical concepts like "consubstantiality" (the idea that the different persons of the Godhead are one in substance). Many in the modern Church of Jesus Christ of Latter-day Saints try to dissolve the aura of paradox by drawing a distinction between the one "Godhead" and the three persons. But the Book of Mormon never invokes explicitly the concept of a Godhead. For Alma and Amulek themselves, it is enough to know that the one God is/are three distinct persons. No effort is made to build a theology around it or to rationalize it. Here again, in Alma's utter lack of concern with providing a theological rationale for the "one God" doctrine, we see an indication that Alma's emphasis is consistently on faith and orthopraxy (correct action), not orthodoxy (correct belief).

2. In the Book of Mormon, the phrase "one God" is only ever used when affirming the unity of the Father, the Son, and the Holy Ghost. In addition to 2 Ne. 31:21, see Mosiah 15:3-5, and Mormon 7:7. Alma had made no mention of "one God" in his sermon to the Zoramites up until that point. So it is a peculiar question to ask unless the Zoramites mean to invoke the earlier controversy.

3. See Alma 33:13–16.

4. See 1 Ne. 17:40–42. This detail is not found in the Biblical account in Numbers.

5. King Hezekiah later destroyed the brass serpent for just this reason; see 2 Kings 18:4

6. When Moses "raised up" the serpent "in the wilderness," Alma notes, "few understood the meaning of those things, and this because of the hardness of their hearts." (33:19-20; see Num. 21:8-9)

7. Put differently, you could say that in passages such as these, "eternal," "endless," and "infinite" are adjectives rather than adverbs. They are characteristics of things; not qualifiers that describe how long an action lasts. Compare D&C 19.

6

1. Christ himself describes "the bowels of mercy" in this way: "He said unto them: Behold, my bowels are filled with compassion towards you. Have ye any that are sick among you? Bring them hither. Have ye any that are lame, or blind, or halt, or maimed, or leprous, or that are withered, or that are deaf, or that are afflicted in any manner? Bring them hither and I will heal them, for I have compassion upon you; my bowels are filled with mercy" (3 Ne. 17:6–7).

7

1. See, e.g., St. Anselm, *Proslogion*, trans. Thomas Williams (Indianapolis, IN: Hackett, 2001), ch. 9, p. 11.

2. Strictly speaking, this is a necessary but not a sufficient condition of a just act. This is because it is not just to give one person what she deserves if at the same time I deprive someone else of what he deserves. A just act makes the world more just, or at least does not make it less just. But for simplicity's sake, I'll ignore this refinement.

3. My thinking about mercy has been heavily influenced by Ned Markosian, "Two Puzzles About Mercy," *The Philosophical Quarterly* 63 (2013): 269–92, and the schema I set out here is indebted to his analysis of mercy.

4. For more on the paradox of deserved forgiveness, see my "Religion and the Transformation of Existence," in *Phenomenology and Human Existence* (Oxford: Oxford University Press, forthcoming 2021).

5. *Oxford English Dictionary,* s.v. "sway." OED Online. Oxford University Press, June 2020, www.oed.com/view/Entry/195582. Accessed 31 August 2020.

PART III

8

1. John Milton, *Christian Doctrine,* in *Complete Prose Works of John Milton*, vol. 6 (New Haven: Yale University Press, 1973), 399.

2. As it does just a few verses prior, where Lehi discusses the ends— i.e., the purposes—of the law and of the atonement (see 2 Ne 2:10).

9

1. In the original chapter breaks of the Book of Mormon, these four modern chapters comprised a single chapter—chapter 19.

2. This does not necessarily mean that God is not "in" time, just that to an immortal being it does not matter how longs things last, or whether they happen now or in the distant future. For us mortals, by contrast, time is of the essence.

3. The rest of the serpent's promise was also a lie. They did not in fact become like the gods in that very day. They perhaps became capable of a godlike understanding of good and evil. But, as history has shown, all too few humans ever actualize this capacity.

4. The idea of a first resurrection is perhaps first hinted at in Jacob 4: 11, but Abinadi is the first to discuss the notion explicitly.

5. John Milton, *Christian Doctrine*, in *Complete Prose Works of John Milton*, vol. 6 (New Haven: Yale University Press, 1973), 400–1.

6. Milton, *Christian Doctrine*, 410.

7. Milton, *Christian Doctrine*, 401.

8. Martin Luther, *The Works of Martin Luther*, ed. Jaroslav Pelikan, vol. 15 (Charlottesville: Fortress Press, 1972), 150.

9. In the Book of Mormon, *soul* typically refers to the living union of spirit and body. See 2 Ne. 9:13; see also D&C 88:15. But Alma seems here to be using *soul* as a synonym for *spirit*. See, for example, Alma 40:19.

10. *American Dictionary of the English Language*, 1st ed. (1828), s.v. "proper." http://webstersdictionary1828.com/Dictionary/proper.

10

1. The word *remorse* appears only three times in the Book of Mormon, and all three instances are in Alma. The disclosive aspect of remorse is suggested by the context of its use in the book of Alma. If their "souls [are] filled with guilt and remorse," Alma tells the people of Zarahemla, it makes them liars when they say "our works have been righteous works upon the face of the earth" (Alma 5:18, 17). In the "Psalm of Alma," Alma ties remorse and joy to the knowledge of good and evil: "He that knoweth good and evil, to him it is given according to his desires...joy or remorse of conscience" (Alma 29:5).

2. *Oxford English Dictionary,* s.v. "typify, v." OED Online, Oxford University Press, June 2020, www.oed.com/view/Entry/208374.

3. *Oxford English Dictionary,* s.v. "type, n." OED Online, Oxford University Press, June 2020, www.oed.com/view/Entry/208330.

4. *Oxford English Dictionary,* s.v. "type."

5. I've followed the emendations in the critical text, based on the original manuscript. See Royal Skousen, ed. *Analysis of Textual Variants of the Book of Mormon, part 4, Critical Text of the Book of Mormon* (Provo, UT: Foundation for Ancient Research and Mormon Studies [FARMS], 2014); also available at https://interpreterfoundation.org/books/atv/p4/

Index

152

TOPICS

156

160

Colophon

The text of the book is typeset in Arnhem,
Fred Smeijer's 21st-century-take on late
18th-century Enlightenment-era letterforms
known for their sturdy legibility and clarity
of form. Captions and figures are typeset in
Quaadraat Sans, also by Fred Smeijers.
The book title and chapter titles are typeset
in Thema by Nikola Djurek.

Printed on Domtar Lynx 74 gsm,
Forest Stewardship Council (FSC) Certified.

Printed by Brigham Young University Print & Mail Services

Woodcut illuminations Brian Kershisnik
Illumination consultation Faith Heard

Book design & typography Douglas Thomas
Production typesetting Maria Camargo

Alma 32:33 And now, behold, because ye have tried the experiment, and planted the seed, and it swelleth and sprouteth, and beginneth to grow, ye must needs know that the seed is good.